T H E

Watch-House

of the Sun

BERKLEY BOOKS BY WAYNE LEE JONES

Weave a Garment of Brightness
God, Good Morning!
The Watch-House of the Sun

THE

Watch-House of the Sun

VIEWS OF HEAVEN FROM THE RELIGIONS OF THE WORLD

Wayne Lee Jones

B

BERKLEY BOOKS, NEW YORK

This book is an original publication of
The Berkley Publishing Group.

THE WATCH-HOUSE OF THE SUN

A Berkley Book / published by arrangement with the author

PRINTING HISTORY
Berkley trade paperback edition / January 1998

The Putnam Berkley World Wide Web site address is
http://www.berkley.com

ISBN: 0-425-16157-9

BERKLEY®
Berkley Books are published by The Berkley Publishing Group,
a member of Penguin Putnam Inc.,
200 Madison Avenue, New York, New York 10016.
BERKLEY and the "B" design
are trademarks belonging to Berkley Publishing Corporation.

PRINTED IN THE UNITED STATES OF AMERICA

10   9   8   7   6   5   4   3   2   1

This book is dedicated to

Krista Lynne Jacobs:

your eyes are, for me, a sufficient heaven.

Rabia' al-Adawiyya prayed:
"Lord,
if I worship You out of hope for Paradise,
deny it to me.
If I worship you out of fear of the Fire,
cast me into it . . . ."

CONTENTS

INTRODUCTION

XI

CHRISTIANITY

I

JUDAISM

55

ISLAM

81

BUDDHISM

99

HINDUISM

113

Contents

ZOROASTRIANISM

127

BAHĀ'I

139

THE ANCIENT WORLD

147

NATIVE TRADITIONS

165

ACKNOWLEDGMENTS

187

◦✧ x ✧◦

INTRODUCTION

S omeday everything we know will pass into oblivion. All the places we have lived, the people we have loved, will turn in time to dust and disappear. Nothing we cling to in this life will endure forever. Eventually all of it, even this planet itself, will vanish.

But where does it go? Will it all simply cease to be, lost like a dream we forget when we awaken? For most of us, this is not a satisfactory answer. We know intuitively that this life is not the only one. Though we cannot remember it, we understand that we were *somewhere* before we were born; though we could not point the way, we know that after the end of our terrestrial lives we will find ourselves in some other place, some other mode of existence. The religions of the world have spoken to this intuition, developed it, and imparted to us the concept of heaven.

What is heaven? This book is an attempt to present some of the many and varied answers that have been offered in response to that question. The materials in this collection are drawn from the major religions of the world, as well as from ancient and indigenous traditions which, too, possess ideas about the nature of heaven. The selections provided in this book are extremely diverse; in fact, upon a first reading, many of them may seem to have nothing in common at all. Yet beneath the specific details, certain patterns may be detected which help explain why heaven has been, and continues to be, so important to so many people.

Heaven, in the framework of this anthology, is a place of peace and abundance, which is home to those who have passed on from this world. Those who are still living their earthly lives might visit heaven, but they cannot stay permanently. It is a place provided specifically for the dead.

Though some claim to have had concrete experiences of the afterlife, for most of us heaven exists only as a hope or a dream. We cannot demonstrate its existence, yet we seem to know it is there. The roots of our conviction in heaven may lie in understandings we obtain from life in this world, and in fundamentally human attitudes and emotions.

Introduction

The thought of our own mortality is tremendously frightening. Loneliness in this world is scary enough; how much more so the idea that we will never see our loved ones again, that we will no longer breathe air nor feel the sun nor laugh with our friends. At the most basic level, the concept of heaven allows us to believe that after we depart from this world we will move to another. The idea that those we cared for go on to a safe and joyous place when they leave us is comforting. And if we are going to believe in a world beyond the one we know, why shouldn't it be better than the one we are used to, full of all the things we never got to have in our earthly lives?

It also seems pointless to many of us to live our entire lives, working as hard as we do—building homes and relationships and families—only to have everything disappear in an instant. The idea that a heaven awaits where we will see the true fruition of our labors and experience the enjoyment of rest in the company of those we have loved, provided with all that we desire, lends meaning to the lives we are leading now. For those whose lives in this world are heavy with pain, sickness, or hardship, the idea that a heaven of rest and relief awaits provides comfort and consolation.

For people who live their lives in accordance with religious observances or moral codes, there is the issue of compensation. If there is to be no reward after death, why bother to live a generous, honest, and noble life here and now? Why not just live for self-gratification, regardless of the hurt done to others or to ourselves? For many people, the rewards of a joyous eternity in heaven justify the efforts of pure living in this world. From a different perspective, we see in ourselves a desire to be distinguished from those who harm us, and who do evil. Will there ever be a place where there is no hurt, no pain, no fear? Heaven is such a place, where the good are kept safe from the bad. No one can take away what delights you in heaven; there, no one can cause you disappointment or make you afraid.

There are so many human reasons to yearn for a heaven that it is no wonder that it has become an important topic in so many religions. Throughout this book, the various selections will not only provide insights into the thinking of various religions, but into the hopes and fears of the human beings who live and believe them. At the root of all speculation about heaven is the meaning of what it is to be human in this world: working toward and dreaming of a day which will be brighter than any we have known.

CHRISTIANITY

The Christian tradition includes perhaps the widest range of descriptions of heaven among all of the world's religions. The combination of a concept of salvation and an absence of explicit and detailed descriptions of the afterlife in the Gospels has encouraged speculation throughout the history of Christianity as to the fate of the soul after death. The numerous sects and movements within Christianity, as well as a number of remarkable individuals, have each contributed their own particular vision of the nature of heaven to the religion.

The Christian heaven is a place of reward for the righteous. There are very few formulations of the Christian afterlife concept which do not juxtapose heaven with hell, a place of punishment for the wicked. Though there are numerous opinions within Christianity as to how one reaches heaven, there is general agreement that not everyone does. Heaven and hell are both eternal in Christianity; the reward of the righteous and the punishment of the wicked go on forever.

Among the themes which frequently recur in Christian descriptions of heaven are visions of God and celestial beings, the absence of sin or evil, endless abundance and joy, and the cessation of reproduction. Christian descriptions also generally concur that heaven is experienced in a spiritual body, rather than in a physical one. These themes are not, however, universal. Some sects of Christianity have adopted the idea that heaven is an indefinite perpetuation of physical life, while others have conceived of a place of pure consciousness or intellect. Furthermore, religious movements such as Mormonism—sometimes associated with Christianity, but distinct from the mainstream Catholic, Orthodox, and Protestant traditions—have developed their own understandings of heaven based on alternative views of the nature of salvation and of the human soul.

The selections in the following section have been chosen to illustrate the variety of descriptions of heaven which have appeared in the Christian context. They speak to many different needs and interests, and are the work of many individuals and communities. Yet, behind the

apparent differences, it is hoped that the reader will perceive the common human thread uniting these visions,
the human hopes and concerns that have motivated
Christians to ponder the question of the fate of the soul
after death.

The following passage, an American work from the early nineteenth century, is representative of a line of Christian speculation which derives its descriptions of heaven from the interpretation of scattered passages throughout the Old and New Testaments. Biblical images such as the "tree of life" and the "throne of the God of glory" are employed to show the description has authoritative roots in Scripture.

The shining firmament, with all the luminaries that adorn it, are but the frontispiece to the highest heaven. All the lustre of diamonds, the fire of carbuncles and rubies, the brightness of pearls are dead in comparison of its glory. It is the throne of the God of glory, wherein his Majesty is revealed in the most illustrious manner. For pleasantness it is called paradise, in allusion to the delightful garden planted by the hands of God himself for Adam, his favorite while innocent. There is the tree of life. There are rivers of pleasure springing from the divine presence. It is called "the inheritance of the saints in light," to signify the glory and joy of the place; for light has a splendour which imparts cheerfulness, and is a fine emblem of both. . . . Heaven for stability is called "a city that has foundations, whose builder and Maker is God." The present world is like a tent or tabernacle set up for a time, while the church is passing through the wilderness; but heaven is "the city of the living God," the place of his happy residence, the seat of his eternal empire. The visible world with all its perishing idols shall shortly fall, this beautiful scene shall be abolished; but the supreme heaven is above the sphere of mutability, wherein all bodies compounded of the jarring elements are continually changing and dissolving. It is truly called "a kingdom that cannot be shaken." The wise Maker has framed it correspondingly to the end for which it was designed; it is the seat of his Majesty, his sacred temple in which he diffuses the richest beams of his goodness and glory, and his chosen servants see and praise his adorable excellencies for ever.

—WILLIAM BATES, *Four Last Things*

This description, published in a book by the Unitarian minister George Weaver around the turn of the twentieth century, points out the similarity of heaven to earth in the respect that humans will retain their individual personalities. It is a statement of the transcendent origin of human qualities and virtues and emphasizes the goodness of human beings, a characteristic belief of the Unitarian movement, and in general of the growth of a Protestantism based on social reform and activism.

Many religious teachers in the past have conceived of heaven as a place of uniformity, and have expected to find a great white throne in the centre, around which are ranged multitudes on multitudes of its people, in rows of equal and exultant saints, with harps in their hands and crowns on their heads, praising God because he has permitted them to stand there, instead of casting them down to hell. Such a heaven must be so tiresome in its monotony and so ill-adapted to human wants, that it cannot be anticipated with pleasure. In this world men are varied in the makeup of their souls and the experience of their lives, so that no two are alike. Each one has a personality and character of his own. Each one must go into the next life in his own personality. The variety of men in that world must be as great as in this. In changing worlds many things will, doubtless, be left behind, but not any one's personality. That is perpetual. Men will go to that world, too, in the variety of character in which they leave this. Death is said to be a leveller, but it does not level character or personality. Men will go into that world as they leave this, but will still be subject to change, to enlightenment, persuasion, reform, growth; for these belong to their spiritual nature.

—GEORGE SUMNER WEAVER, *Heaven*

This passage, written in 1728, is an excerpt from the most famous work of William Law, an Anglican clergyman who retired to contemplation and ascetic practices in the latter part of his life. Law insists that death is not to be feared; the delight of the experience of heaven surpasses the pain or grief which may accompany the journey toward it.

For what is there miserable or dreadful in death, but the consequences of it? When a man is dead, what does anything signify to him, but the state he is then in? Our poor friend Lepidus died, you know, as he was dressing himself for a feast; do you think it is now part of his trouble that he did not live till that entertainment was over? Feasts and business and pleasures and enjoyments seem great things to us whilst we think of nothing else; but as soon as we add death to them, they all sink into an equal littleness; and the soul that is separated from the body no more laments the loss of business than the losing of a feast.

If I am now going into the joys of God, could there be any reason to grieve that this happened to me before I was forty years of age? Could it be a sad thing to go to Heaven before I had made a few more bargains, or stood a little longer behind a counter? And if I am to go amongst lost spirits, could there be any reason to be content that this did not happen to me till I was old and full of riches? If good angels were ready to receive my soul, could it be any grief to me that I was dying upon a poor bed in a garret? And if God had delivered me up to evil spirits, to be dragged by them to places of torments, could it be any comfort to me that they found me upon a bed of state? When you are as near death as I am, you will know that all the different states of life, whether of youth or age, riches or poverty, greatness or meanness, signify no more to you than whether you die in a poor or stately apartment. The greatness of those things which follow death makes all that goes before it sink into nothing.

—WILLIAM LAW,
A Serious Call to a Devout and Holy Life

Clive Staples Lewis (known also as C. S. Lewis), 1898–1963, was an English scholar of medieval and Renaissance literature, as well as an apologist for conservative Christianity and an Anglican theologian. In this passage Lewis offers a beautiful explanation of the Christian idea that physical sexuality is not a part of heaven.

The letter and spirit of Scripture, and of all Christianity, forbid us to suppose that life in the New Creation will be a sexual life; and this reduces our imagination to the withering alternative either of bodies which are hardly recognizable as human bodies at all or else of a perpetual fast. As regards the fast, I think our present outlook might be like that of a small boy who, on being told that the sexual act was the highest bodily pleasure, should immediately ask whether you ate chocolates at the same time. On receiving the answer "No," he might regard the absence of chocolates as the chief characteristic of sexuality. In vain would you tell him that the reason why lovers in their carnal raptures don't bother about chocolates is that they have something better to think of. The boy knows chocolate: He does not know the positive thing that excludes it. We are in the same position. We know the sexual life; we do not know, except in glimpses, the other things which, in Heaven, will leave no room for it. Hence where fullness awaits us we anticipate fasting. In denying that sexual life, as we now understand it, makes any part of the final beatitude, it is not, of course, necessary to suppose that the distinction of sexes will disappear. What is no longer needed for biological purposes may be expected to survive for splendor. Sexuality is the instrument both of virginity and conjugal virtue; neither men nor women will be asked to throw away weapons they have used victoriously. It is the beaten and the fugitives who throw away their swords. The conquerors sheathe theirs and retain them. . . . I am well aware that this last . . . may seem to many readers unfortunate and to some comic. But that very comedy, as I must repeatedly insist, is the symptom of our estrangement, as spirits, from Nature and our estrangement, as animals, from Spirit. The whole conception of the New Creation involves the belief that this estrangement will be healed. A curious consequence will follow. The archaic type of thought which could not clearly distinguish spiritual "Heaven" from the sky, is from our point of view a confused type of thought. But it also resembles and anticipates a type of thought which will one day be true. That archaic sort of thinking will become simply the correct sort when Nature and Spirit and fully harmonized—when Spirit rides Nature so perfectly that the two together make rather a Centaur than a mounted knight. I do not mean necessarily that the blending of Heaven and sky, in particular, will turn out to be specially true, but that that kind of blending will accurately mirror the reality which will then exist. There will be no room to get the finest razor blade of thought in between Spirit and Nature.

—C. S. LEWIS, *Miracles: A Preliminary Study*

In this selection, George Weaver offers his answer to the concern of parents for the fate of children who die in their youth. In the course of his answer, the author presents a heaven of growth, work, and change; a heaven reflecting the American ideal of progress which influenced the development of Protestantism in the United States.

"Will children who die in infancy grow in heaven?" This is a mother question, a love question, asked by many anxious parents, and asked in these exact words, of the author, by a mother who had given four infant children to heaven. No question of religion or life is more momentous to her than this, touching the condition of her little ones in heaven. She expects to meet them there; but will they be grown up to know and enjoy her as their mother and nearest friend? is her query, and the query of every mother under like circumstances. It has been said that half the human race die in childhood. However this may be, we know that many die before maturity. If they do not grow and mature in heaven, what a world of infants that must be! The very thought of it is so objectionable that we cannot entertain it with complacency. It is in the nature of the young mind to mature. It does not change its nature in laying off its robe of flesh. Growth is not in the flesh so much as in the spirit. . . . Nothing else, therefore, can be expected of infant children but that they will grow in heaven in mental stature and power, till they shall reach maturity; and then grow in knowledge, wisdom, and worth, as men and women do. It would seem more probable, almost certain, that the heavenly inhabitants would institute means to nourish the young mind in its growth—such means as are suggested by our homes, kindergartens, and schools; only better. The mind must be even more trainable there than here, because it is away from the earthly hindrances and in its natural and kindred environment. Fathers and mothers and teachers are there in vast numbers, and the parental element is in all its inhabitants, to do what they can to promote a sound and harmonious growth of the young souls which are to be their companions forever. What a privilege it will be for them to join in the educational work of heaven, and be thus associated with the rising generations of the angelic hosts! Not a little of the joy of heaven will come to parent souls in this employment of their time and powers in the service of children and youth.

—GEORGE SUMNER WEAVER, *Heaven*

The scholar and theologian C. S. Lewis is most famous for his series of children's books, The Chronicles of Narnia. *These books use an imaginative setting to explain concepts of Christian living and describe the Second Coming of Christ and the afterlife. In the selection below, taken from the final book of the series, Lewis offers a metaphor for the difference between heavenly and earthly existence.*

It is as hard to explain how this sunlit land was different from the old Narnia, as it would be to tell you how the fruits of that country taste. Perhaps you will get some idea of it, if you think like this. You may have been in a room in which there was a window that looked out on a lovely bay of the sea or a green valley that wound away among mountains. And in the wall of that room opposite to the window there may have been a looking glass. And as you turned away from the window suddenly caught sight of that sea or that valley, all over again, in the looking glass. And the sea in the mirror, or the valley in the mirror, were in one sense just the same as the real ones: Yet at the same time they were somehow different—deeper, more wonderful, more like places in a story: in a story you have never heard but very much want to know. The difference between the old Narnia and the new Narnia was like that. The new one was a deeper country: Every rock and flower and blade of grass looked as if it meant more. I can't describe it any better than that: If you ever get there, you will know what I mean. It was the Unicorn who summed up what everyone was feeling. He stamped his right fore-hoof on the ground and neighed and then cried: "I have come home at last! This is my real country! I belong here. This is the land I have been looking for all my life, though I never knew it till now. The reason why we loved the old Narnia is that it sometimes looked a little like this. Bree-hee-hee! Come further up, come further in!" He shook his mane and sprang forward into a great gallop—a Unicorn's gallop which, in our world, would have carried him out of sight in a few moments. But now a most strange thing happened. Everyone else began to run, and they found, to their astonishment, that they could keep up with him: not only the Dogs and the humans but even fat little Puzzle and short-legged Poggin the Dwarf. The air flew in their faces as if they were driving fast in a car without a windscreen. The country flew past as if they were seeing it from the windows of an express train. Faster and faster they raced, but no one got hot or tired or out of breath.

—C. S. LEWIS, *The Last Battle*

This selection, written by an American theologian in the middle of the nineteenth century, points out that if certain basic concepts accepted by many Christians about heaven are true, then the experience of heaven must be so different from that of earthly life that it is almost entirely beyond our comprehension.

It is clear that our economy of life will be entirely changed. If there shall be a material economy in any degree resembling this present organization of earth, air, fire, and water, it will, in some important respects, be entirely unlike the present. At present accidents, resulting from the density of matter, and from the laws of gravitation, are inevitable. Under the present organization, the elements are hostile to man. In heaven, it is declared, there shall be no more pain, no darkness, no need of the sun, and no more sea. In heaven there can be no more decay, for into that holy place there entereth nothing which defileth; yet we are led to believe that there will be an endless variety in scenery. But how this can be, without those changes which are now inseparable from decay, we are unable to conceive. If there be no decay, how can there be a renewal of vegetation? And if no renewal of vegetation, apparently there can be no succession of seasons. And as our present enjoyment, and even our life itself, is completely formed upon the succession of the seasons, it becomes entirely plain that there must be a change so radical and so entire, as to baffle all present attempts to grasp the actual future.

—JAMES WILLIAM KIMBALL, *Heaven*

In this passage, Protestant preacher William Branks appeals to the emotions of Christian believers, offering hope for the future life. It presents an idea which has captivated many Christians: Heaven is the true and natural home of the human soul, and heavenly life consists in sharing in the love and acceptance of an eternal, spiritual community.

Or it may be that you are confined to your sick-chamber, and are now laid down upon your bed of death.... The rising sun is just beginning to pour his brightening beams into your sorrowful dwelling, shadowing forth to your friends around you the morning of a glorious eternity that is bursting out with its flood of light upon your waning eye. You shake hands with your weeping relatives, who are at your bedside, like an individual setting out upon a long journey, or embarking in an emigrant vessel; and you bid them an affectionate farewell. You have taken the last look of the home you are about to leave, and of the well-known, dear, but sorrowful faces that are around you; your spirit is struggling to be free; angels are hovering over you in their sympathy and love, waiting till the last spasm with you is over, that they may conduct you in triumph to the realms of life, to the brightness of eternal day. Is your name enrolled in the Book of Life? Are you a child of God? How comforting to you, in your present circumstances, is the knowledge that heaven is your home! Death to you will thus merely take you out of one home, that it may usher you into another.... It is a passage from the midst of the warm, loving bosoms of the present members of your family, who are dear to you, up into heaven, to become associated for eternity with the warmer and more loving bosoms of God's great family, who are waiting for you to join their happy number with songs of unspeakable joy.

—WILLIAM BRANKS, *Heaven Our Home*

The Watch-House of the Sun

<hr />

Emanuel Swedenborg, 1688–1772, was a Swedish scientist and phi-
losopher who rejected many traditional Christian beliefs, such as orig-
inal sin. He had a mystical experience in the middle of his life,
during which he claimed to have seen the true nature of the spiritual
and physical worlds and literally entered both heaven and hell. Swe-
denborg believed that heaven was not a reward, but rather the in-
evitable consequence of a life of preparation and self-development. His
description of heaven is voluminous; the passage below, which deals
with the type of writing used in heaven, is one small example from
his unusual and complicated work.

A bit of paper was once sent me from heaven, on
which were written only a few words in the Hebrew
character: and I was told that every letter involved arcana of wisdom, and that those arcana were contained
in the inflexions and curvatures of the letters, and
thence likewise in the sounds. From this was made
plain to me the meaning of the Lord's words: "Verily
I say unto you, till heaven and earth pass, one iota or
little horn shall not pass from the law," Matt. v. 18.
That the Word is divine as to every tittle thereof, is
also known in the church. But where the Divine lies
concealed in every tittle, is not yet known; wherefore it
shall be declared. The writing in the inmost heaven
consists of various inflected and circumflected forms;
and the inflexions and circumflexions are according to

the form of heaven. By these the angels express the arcana of their wisdom, many of which cannot be expressed in words; and, what is wonderful, the angels are skilled in such writing without being taught. It is implanted in them like their speech.

This kind of writing, by means of characters of a heavenly form, is in use in the inmost heaven where they excel all others in wisdom. By those characters they express the affections from which their thoughts flow and follow in order according to the subject treated of. Hence those writings involve arcana which no thought can exhaust. I have also been permitted to see them. But there are no such writings in the inferior heavens. The writings there are like those in the world, in similar letters, yet not intelligible to man because they are in angelic language, which has nothing in common with human languages, for by the vowels they express affections, by the consonants, the ideas of thought proceeding from those affections, and by the words composed of both, the meaning they wish to convey. This kind of writing also involves in a few words more than a man can record in several pages. I have seen writings of this kind also. In this manner they have the Word written in the inferior heavens; and in the inmost heavens they have it written in heavenly characters.

—EMANUEL SWEDENBORG,
*Heaven and Its Wonders
and Hell from Things Seen and Heard*

The Watch~House of the Sun

❦

"St. Brendan's Voyage" is an early medieval description of a journey supposedly taken by the historical St. Brendan. In the course of the journey St. Brendan visits heaven, which is an actual island in the midst of the Atlantic ocean. It is a delightful story, probably gleaned from folktales, Church legends, and the stories of actual sailors, reflecting the combination of popular myths with theological concepts.

After an hour had passed a great light shone around them, and the boat stood by the shore.

When they disembarked, they saw an extensive land thickly set with trees, laden with fruit, as in the autumn. All the time they were crossing that land, during their stay in it, there was no night. A light always shone, like the light of the sun in the meridian, and for the forty days they viewed the land in various directions, but could not find its borders. One day, however, they came to a large river flowing towards the middle of the land, which they could not cross in any way. St. Brendan then said to the brethren, "We cannot cross this river, and we must therefore remain ignorant of the size of this country." While they were considering this matter, a young man of brightly shining features and very handsome appearance came to them and joyfully embracing and addressing each of them by his own name said, "Peace be with you, brothers, and with all who practise the peace of Christ. Blessed are they, O Lord, who live in your house. They will praise you forever and ever." He then said to St. Brendan, "This is the land you have sought after for so long, but you could not find it before now because Christ our Lord wished first to show you his various mysteries in this immense ocean. Return now to the land of your birth, bearing with you as much of those fruits and precious stones as your boat can carry, for the days of your earthly pilgrimage must draw to a close, when you can rest in peace among your saintly brethren. After many years this land will be shown to those who come after you, when days of tribulation come upon the people of Christ. The great river you see here divides this land into two parts, and just as it appears now, teeming with ripe fruits, so it always remains, without any blight or shadow whatever, for unfailing light shines on it." When St. Brendan inquired whether this land would be revealed to all, the young man replied, "When the most high Creator has brought all nations under subjection, then this land will be made known to all his elect." Soon after, St. Brendan received the blessing of this man and prepared for his return to his own country. He gathered some of the fruits of the land and various kinds of precious stones, and taking a last farewell of the good provider who had each year supplied food for him and his brethren, he embarked once more and sailed back through the darkness again.

—"St. Brendan's Voyage"

─────

The selection below is an excerpt from "Tundale's Vision," a medieval Irish description of heaven that specifies particular rewards in heaven for particular good deeds on earth. The good souls mentioned in this particular passage are being rewarded for their support and defense of churches.

When Tundale's soul wished to remain here with these sweet visions, the angel said to him, "Look back." And looking back he saw a great and wide tree with leaves and flowers very green and fertile with all types of fruit. In its leaves lingered many birds of different colors and of different voices, singing and making music. Underneath its branches very many lillies and roses sprang up, and varieties of all herbs and species produced perfumes. Under the same tree there were many men and women in gold and ivory shrines, and without ceasing they praised the omnipotent God for all his goodness and his gifts, and all of them had gold crowns wonderfully decorated on their heads and held scepters of gold in their hands, and they were dressed with robes like the monks before wore.

The soul turned to the angel and said, "Spirit, what tree is this, and who are those under it? What good did they do when they were alive?" And the angel said, "This tree is a figure of the Holy Church. These who are under it are men and women, builders and defenders of the church, who tried either to build or defend churches. And they gave their goods abundantly to holy churches. They followed the brotherhood and community of those who leave the habit of the world and restrain themselves from the carnal desires that fight against the soul. Sober and just and pious they lived in this world, looking forward to blessed hope which, as you see, did not disappoint them." And the angel said, "Let us go on."

—"Tundale's Vision"

John Bunyan, the author of the classic Pilgrim's Progress, *was an English Puritan who spent much of his life in prison for his resistance to religious authority. Bunyan's depiction of heaven emphasizes the absence of evil and temptation and its replacement with clear vision and understanding. The account is most interesting in that it explains what is desirable about heaven by indicating what is undesirable about this world.*

First then, the souls of all the blessed here are freed for ever from whatsoever it is can make them miserable; the chief of which, you are not ignorant, is sin: It is only that which bring the creature into misery, and entails it on him. But, secondly, as here the blessed souls are freed from sin, so are they likewise from all occasions of it;

which is a great addition to our happiness. No devil here can tempt them, nor no corruption enter: Nothing but what is pure and holy can find admission here: No sly suggestions from that apostate spirit can molest us here. Nor shall the world be any more a tempter to those blessed souls, who have through faith and patience overcome its wiles, and arrived safely here. As strong as its temptations and allurements are to saints themselves, who are still miliating with it in the world below, we that are here possessed of heavenly mansions, look with contempt on all terrane enjoyments: We here are got above the world, and all that it can tempt us with: and through the blood of our triumphing Jesus, have got the victory over it, as these bright palms we bear do evidence. There is nothing here that can disturb our peace; but an eternal calm crowns all our happiness being freed from sin and all temptations to it.

These are the things we are in this blessed state delivered from; and yet these make up but the least part of the happiness of Heaven: Our joys are positive as well as privative, and what those are I now proceed to shew you.

We enjoy here the Beatific Vision, the blessed spring and eternal source of our happiness: But what this is, I can no more declare than finite creatures comprehend infinity; only we find that it continually eradiates our understandings, and fills our souls with joy unspeakable and full of glory; and with a love so flaming that nothing but the blessed author of it can satisfy, nor not eternity itself can terminate; it is the reflected brightness of the Divine Presence, and transcendently glorious emanations of his goodness, that is the life of our lives, the soul of our souls, and the heaven of heavens; and that which makes us live, and love, and sing, and praise for ever; and which transforms our souls into his blessed likeness.

Here we enjoy the perfection of all grace: In the world below, the saints see but in part, and know but in part; but here, that which is perfect being enjoyed, that which is imperfect is done away: Below, love is mixed with fear, and fear hath torment; but here, love is perfect, and perfect love casteth out fear: Here we love the blessed God more than ourselves, and one another like ourselves: We here are all the children of one Father, and all our brethren are alike dear unto us.

—"Vision of John Bunyan"

The Watch-House of the Sun

The Divine Comedy, *completed by Dante Alighieri, 1265–1321, in 1321, remains one of the most influential texts in the development of Christian thought about heaven. Its imagery has been incorporated into almost all of the mainstream depictions of the afterlife which followed it. The poem describes Dante's journey through hell, purgatory, and paradise under the guidance of the Roman poet Virgil and, later, his beloved Beatrice. At the end of the poem Dante is granted a vision of the Divine Face. The passage below is taken from Dante's description of the saints in the Heavenly Court.*

Then like to people 'neath a masked disguise
Who others seem than erst, themselves confest
When stript away their semblant fantasies,

So did there change to jubilee increased
The flowers and sparkles that I there beheld
Both Courts of Heaven before me manifest.

O splendour of my God, whence I beheld
The lofty triumph of the truthful reign,
Give me the power to say how I beheld!

Light is above that maketh visible plain
The Maker to the creature, who alone
In seeing Him doth perfect peace attain.

The Watch-House of the Sun

And in a circular shape it rayeth on,
Of such a size that its circumference
Unto the sun would be too large a zone.

Upon the primum mobile it hence
Imprints its semblance with reflected sheen,
Which thence doth draw its lift and influence.

And like a cliff that o'er the wave serene
Mirrors itself, as 'twere, to see how fair
Is all its wealth of flowerets and of green,

So standing o'er the light in circles there
I saw them glassed on more than thousand thrones,
All of our race who thither made repair.

And as the central grade within it owns
So great a light, how vast doth spread in size
This Rose's petals in its furthest zones!

In all its height and amplitude my eyes
Were not bewildered, but took in it all,
The quantity and nature of its joys.

Nearness and distance do not there befall,
For where God rules immediate and supernal
The laws of Nature have no sway at all.

With the yellow of the Rose eternal,
Which opens out in grades and breathes delight
And odorous praise to the sun for ever vernal,

Like one who, silent, fain would speak, forthright
Beatrix led me on, and said, "Behold
How great the gathering of our stoles of white!

Behold what space our city doth enfold!
Behold our seats already so complete
That few more guests we wait to see enrolled.

—DANTE ALIGHIERI, *The Divine Comedy*

<hr />

Gregory I, also known as Saint Gregory the Great, was a doctor of the Church and Pope from 590–604. He set the precedent for the development of the medieval papacy, expanding the temporal powers of the Church and encouraging missionary activity. In the passage below, Saint Gregory answers a particular problem in the interpretation of Scripture and offers an insight into the nature of heavenly reward: The righteous receive enjoyment to the fullness of their individual capacities, but each righteous person has a different capacity. Thus, while not all souls receive the same merit in heaven, each soul reaches its own satisfaction.

And why are the souls of good men and of wicked men separated into groups to live in common dwellings

according to their common status of good or evil?
Christ Himself gives us the answer and His words
would suffice even if we had no examples to cite. He
was speaking in behalf of his chosen ones when He
said, "There are many dwelling places in my Father's
house." If there were no distinction of rewards in that
blessed abode, there should be but one dwelling place,
not many. As it is, the dwelling places in heaven are
numerous in order to keep the ranks of good souls distinct and allow them to enjoy the companionship of
those of like merits. Yet, it is said that all those who
laboured received each a silver piece, though now they
are separated into distinct groups with many dwellings.
The bliss, namely, which they enjoy is one and the
same, but the reward they earn for their different degrees of good is unequal.

—SAINT GREGORY THE GREAT, *Dialogues*

———

*Richard Baxter, 1615–1691, was an English Puritan clergyman
whose descriptions of heaven, such as the following excerpt, received
wide acclaim and readership. His works were classics of popular
religion and exemplify some of the fundamental ideas about heaven
which were incorporated into later Protestantism. The end of formal
religion in heaven described in this passage is a characteristic of the
austere, Puritan attitude toward outward displays of religiosity.*

The rest here in question is, the most happy estate of a Christian, having obtained the end of his course: or, it is the perfect endless fruition of God by the perfected saints, according to the measure of their capacity, to which their souls arrive at death: and both soul and body most fully after the resurrection and final judgment.

There is contained in this rest a cessation from motion or action. Not from all action, but of that which implies the absence of the end. When we have obtained the haven, we have done failing; when we are at our journey's end, we have done with the way. Therefore prophesying ceaseth, tongues fail, and knowledge shall be done away; that is, so far as it was imperfect. There shall be no more prayer, because no more necessity, but the full enjoyment of what we prayed for. Neither shall we need to fast, and weep and watch any more, being out of the reach of sin and temptations. Nor will there be use for instructions and exhortations: preaching is done: the ministry of man ceaseth: sacraments useless: the labourers called in, because the harvest is gathered: the unregenerate past hope, the saints past fear, for ever. Much less shall there be any need of labouring for inferior ends, as here we do; seeing they shall all devolve themselves into the ocean of the ultimate end, and the lesser good be swallowed up in the greatest.

This rest containeth a perfect freedom from all the evils that accompany us through our course, and which necessarily follow our absence from the chief good: besides our freedom from those eternal flames, which the neglecters of Christ must endure. There is no such thing as grief and sorrow known there nor is there such a thing as a pale face, a languid body, feeble joints, unable infancy, decrepit age, peccant humours, painful sickness, gripping fears, consuming care, nor whatsoever deserves the name of evil. Indeed a gale of groans and sighs, a stream of tears, accompanied us to the very gates, and there bid us farewell for ever. We did weep and lament, when the world did rejoice; but our sorrow is turned into joy; and our joy shall no man take from us.

—RICHARD BAXTER, *The Saints' Everlasting Rest*

The next selection bases its description of heaven on logical argument and principles of natural science, a characteristic of Christian apologetics during the Enlightenment. As in many Christian descriptions, there is an emphasis on new abilities and attributes gained upon the attainment of heaven.

We conceive, without difficulty, that our present senses are susceptible of a degree of perfection much superior to what we know them to have here, and which astonishes us on certain subjects. We can even form to ourselves a pretty distinct idea of this increase of perfection, by the prodigious effects of optical and acoustic instruments.

Let us suppose Aristotle observing a mite with our microscopes, or contemplating with our telescopes Jupiter and his moons, what surprise would he not have felt! What shall not we too feel, when clothed in a spiritual body, our senses shall have acquired all the perfection which they can receive from the beneficent author of our being?

We can imagine, if we please, that our eyes will then unite in themselves the qualities of microscopes and telescopes, and that they will accommodate themselves exactly to all distances; and how much superior will the glasses of these new perspectives be to those of which art boasts so much?

Neither is it very difficult for us to conceive, that the germ of the spiritual body may contain at present the organic element of new senses which will not be unfolded till the resurrection.

The new senses will then discover to us in bodies, the properties which must always remain unknown to us here: how many sensible qualities which we are yet ignorant of, and which we shall discover with astonishment! We know the different powers of nature, only by means of their relation to the different senses upon which they exert their action. How many powers are there of which we don't even suspect the existence, because there is no relation between the ideas which we acquire by our five senses, and those which we shall be able to acquire by other senses? Let us imagine a man who should be born with a perfect palsy upon three or four principal senses, and let us suppose natural causes which would give life and motion to these senses, and put them all into a proper state; what a crowd of perceptions, new, various, and unforeseen, would such a man acquire in a little time! What a prodigious increase of improvement would he gain in all his faculties?

These new senses, the infinitely small miniatures of which are enclosed in the seat of the soul, have a direct relation to that future world, our true country.

—CHARLES BONNET,
Conjectures Concerning the Nature of Future Happiness

———

Saint Ephraem, 306–373, was a doctor of the Church and was known for his beautiful metered hymns and homilies. His devotional works are still used in the liturgy of the Nestorian Church. One of his hymns, presented here, describes a heaven divided into various levels for different types of righteous individuals. Saint Ephraem also emphasizes that preparation must be made during earthly life for heaven to be received.

Forge here on earth and take
the key to Paradise;
the Door that welcomes you

smiles radiantly upon you;
the Door, all discerning,
conforms its measure to those who enter it:
in its wisdom
it shrinks and it grows.
According to the stature and rank
attained by each person,
it shows by its dimensions
whether they are perfect, or lacking in something.

When people see
that they have lost everything,
that riches do not endure
and carnal desires no longer exist,
that beauty and power
disappear and vanish,
then they recollect themselves
and are filled with remorse,
because, choked with care,
they heard with contempt those words,
"Your possessions are but a passing dream,
your inheritance, darkness."

The righteous, too, perceive
that their own affliction no longer exists,
their suffering does not endure,
their burden no longer remains,

and it seems as if no anguish
had ever assailed them.
Their fasts appear
as though a mere dream,
for they have woken as it were from sleep
to discover Paradise
and the Kingdom's table
spread out before them.

By those who are outside
the summit cannot be scaled,
but from inside Paradise inclines its whole self
to all who ascend it;
the whole of its interior
gazes upon the just with joy.
Paradise girds the loins
of the world,
encircling the great sea;
neighbor to the beings on high,
friendly to those within it,
hostile to those without.

Who is capable of gazing
upon the Garden's splendor,
seeing how glorious it is in all its design,
how harmonious in its proportions,
how spacious for those who dwell there,

how radiant with its abodes?
Its fountains delight
with their fragrance,
but when they issue forth toward us
they become impoverished in our country,
since they put on the savors
of our land as we drink them.

When the just ascend its various levels
to receive their inheritance,
with justice He raises up each one
to the degree that accords with his labors;
each is stopped at the level
whereof he is worthy,
there being sufficient levels in Paradise
for everyone:
the lowest parts for the repentant,
the middle for the righteous,
the heights for those victorious,
while the summit is reserved for God's Presence.

——SAINT EPHRAEM THE SYRIAN,
Second Hymn on Paradise

⸺⸎⸺

Saint Maximos the Confessor resigned from a post in the government
of the Byzantine Emperor Heraclius to become a monk. During his

life, 580—662, he taught that virtue consisted of the combination of asceticism and charity. In this passage, Saint Maximos shows that heaven may be many things, depending upon the qualities inherent in the individual believer.

Some scholars try to discover how the eternal dwelling-places and things promised differ from each other. Is there a difference in their actual locality? Or does the difference arise from our conception of the spiritual quality and quantity peculiar to each dwelling- place? Some think the first and some the second. He who knows the meaning of "The kingdom of God is within you," and "In my Father's house are many dwelling-places," will prefer the second explanation.

The kingdom of God the Father is present in all believers in potentiality; it is present in actuality in those who, after totally expelling all natural life of soul and body from their inner state, have attained the life of the Spirit alone and are able to say, "I no longer live, but Christ lives in me."

Some say that the kingdom of heaven is the way of life which the saints lead in heaven; others that it is a state similar to that of the angels, attained by those who are saved; others that it is the very form of the divine beauty of those who "wear the image of Him who is from heaven." In my judgment each of these three views is correct. For the grace of the kingdom is given to all according to the quality and quantity of the righteousness that is in them.

——SAINT MAXIMOS THE CONFESSOR, *Philokalia*

———

This selection by Saint Gregory of Sinai, an important figure of the Eastern Orthodox tradition, refers to the view that earthly existence is a corruption of the natural, spiritual state of humankind. Further, there are gradations within the afterlife which correspond to the varying degrees of spiritual perfection found in worshipers. The Philokalia *is a collection of short treatises and sayings by the founders of the Eastern Orthodox Church.*

The kingdom of heaven is like the tabernacle which was built by God, and which He disclosed to Moses as a pattern; for it too has an outer and an inner sanctuary. Into the first will enter all who are priests of grace. But into the second——which is noetic—— will enter only those who in this life have attained the divine darkness of theological wisdom and there as true hierarchs have celebrated the triadic liturgy, entering into the tabernacle that Jesus Himself has set up, where He acts as their consecrator and chief Hierarch before the Trinity, and illumines them ever more richly with His own splendour.

By "many dwelling-places" the Saviour meant the

differing stages of spiritual ascent and states of development in the other world; for although the kingdom of heaven is one, there are many different levels within it. That is to say, there is place for both heavenly and earthly men according to their virtue, their knowledge, and the degree of deification that they have attained. "For there is one glory of the sun, and another glory of the moon, and another glory of the stars, for one star differs from another star in glory"; and yet all of them shine in a single divine firmament.

You partake of angelic life and attain an incorruptible and hence almost bodiless state when you have cleansed your intellect through tears, have through the power of the Spirit resurrected your soul even in this life, and with the help of the Logos have made your flesh— your natural human form of clay—a resplendent and fiery image of divine beauty. For bodies become incorruptible when rid of their natural humours and their material density.

The body in its incorruptible state will be earthy, but it will be without humours or material density, indescribably transmuted from an unspiritual body into a spiritual body, so that it will be in its godlike refinement and subtleness both earthy and heavenly. Its state when it is resurrected will be the same as that in which it was originally created—one in which it conforms to the image of the Son of Man through full participation in His divinity.

The promised land is dispassion, from which spiritual joy flows like milk and honey.

The saints in heaven hold inner converse together, communicating mystically through the power of the Holy Spirit.

If we do not know what we are like when God makes us, we shall not realize what sin has turned us into.

Rewards correspond to labours. But their quantity or quality—that is to say, their measure—will be shown by the position and state in heaven of those who receive them.

According to Scripture, the saints, the sons of Christ's resurrection, through incorruption and deification will become intellects, that is to say, equal to the angels.

It is said that in the life to come the angels and saints ever increase in gifts of grace and never abate their longing for further blessings. No lapse or veering from virtue to vice takes place in that life.

—SAINT GREGORY OF SINAI, *Philokalia*

Saint Augustine of Hippo, 354–430, was one of the most influential thinkers in the history of the Western Church. His famous book The City of God *contrasts a mythical pagan city with an ideal Chris-*

tian city, the latter becoming the model for Augustine's view of heavenly existence.

How great shall be that felicity, which shall be tainted with no evil, which shall lack no good, and which shall afford leisure for the praises of God, who shall be all in all! For I know not what other employment there can be where no lassitude shall slacken activity, nor any want stimulate to labour. I am admonished also by the sacred song, in which I read or hear the words, "Blessed are they that dwell in Thy house, O Lord; they will be still praising Thee." All the members and organs of the incorruptible body, which now we see to be suited to various necessary uses, shall contribute to the praises of God; for in that life necessity shall have no place, but full, certain, secure, everlasting felicity. For all those parts of the bodily harmony, which are distributed through the whole body, within and without, and of which I have just been saying that they at present elude our observation, shall then be discerned; and, along with the other great and marvellous discoveries which shall then kindle rational minds in praise of the great Artificer, there shall be the enjoyment of a beauty which appeals to the reason. What power of movement such bodies shall possess, I have not the audacity rashly to define, as I have not the ability to conceive. Nevertheless I will say that in any case, both in motion and at rest, they shall be, as in their appearance, seemly; for into that state nothing which is unseemly shall be admitted. One thing is certain, the body shall forthwith be wherever the spirit wills, and the spirit shall will nothing which is unbecoming either to the spirit or to the body. True honour shall be there, for it shall be denied to none who is worthy, nor yielded to any unworthy; neither shall any unworthy person so much as sue for it, for none but the worthy shall be there. True peace shall be there, where no one shall suffer opposition either from himself or any other. God Himself, who is the Author of virtue, shall be its reward; for, as there is nothing greater or better, He has promised Himself. What else was meant by His word through the prophet, "I will be your God, and ye shall be my people," than, I shall be their satisfaction, I shall be all that men honourably desire—life, and health, and nourishment, and plenty, and glory, and honour, and peace, and all good things? This, too, is the right interpretation of the saying of the apostle, "That God may be all in all." He shall be the end of our desires who shall be seen without end, loved without cloy, praised without weariness. This outgoing of affection, this employment, shall certainly be, like eternal life itself, common to all.

But who can conceive, not to say describe, what degrees of honour and glory shall be awarded to the various degrees of merit? Yet it cannot be doubted that there shall be degrees. And in that blessed city there shall be this great blessing, that no inferior shall envy

any superior, as now the archangels are not envied by
the angels, because no one will wish to be what he has
not received, though bound in strictest concord with
him who has received; as in the body the finger does
not seek to be the eye, though both members are har-
moniously included in the complete structure of the
body. And thus, along with this gift, greater or less,
each shall receive this further gift of contentment to
desire no more than he has.

—SAINT AUGUSTINE OF HIPPO, *The City of God*

―――∞∞∞―――

*Quintus Septimius Florens Tertullianus, commonly known as
Tertullian, lived in the third century, a Father of the Church and a
bishop of Carthage. He was the author of a number of important
apologetic and doctrinal works, and a number of texts are attributed
to him. The verse below is traditionally ascribed to Tertullian, though
it may be the work of another bishop of Carthage, Verecundus. It is
a vivid description of heaven, unusual in that it primarily relies upon
sensual imagery to convey the beauty of the afterlife.*

A place there is, beloved of the Lord,
In Eastern coasts, where light is bright and clear,
And healthier blows the breeze; day is eterne,
Time changeless: 'tis a region set apart
By God, most rich in plains, and passing blest,

In the meridian of His cloudess seat.
There gladsome is the air, and is in light
Ever to be; soft is the wind, and breathes
Life-giving blasts; earth, fruitful with a soil
Luxuriant, bears all things; in the meads
Flowers shed their fragrance; and upon the plains
The purple—not in envy—mingles all
With golden-ruddy light. One gladsome flower,
With its own lustre clad, another clothes;
And here with many a seed the dewy fields
Are dappled, and the snowy tilths are crisped
With rosy flowers. No region happier
Is known in other spots; none which in look
Is fairer, or in honour more excels.
Never in flowery gardens are there born
Such lilies, nor do such upon our plains
Outbloom; nor does the rose so blush, what time,
New-born, 'tis opened by the breeze; nor is
The purple with such hue by Tyrian dye
Imbued. With coloured pebbles beauteous gleams
The gem: here shines the prasinus; there glows
The carbuncle; and giant-emerald
Is green with grassy light. Here too are born
The cinnamons, with odoriferous twigs;
And with dense leaf gladsome amomum joins
Its fragrance. Here, a native, lies the gold
Of radiant sheen; and lofty groves reach heaven
In blooming time, and germens fruitfullest

Burden the living boughs. No glades like these
Hath Ind herself forth-stretcht; no tops so dense
Rears on her mount the pine; nor with a shade
So lofty-leaved is her cypress crisped;
Nor better in its season blooms her bough
In spring-tide. Here black firs on lofty peak
Bloom; and the only woods that know no hail
Are green eternally: no foliage falls;
At no time fails the flower. There, too, there blooms
A flower as red as Tarsine purple is:
A rose, I ween, it is (red hue it has,
And odour keen); such aspect on its leaves
It wears, such odour breathes. A tree it stands,
With a new flower, fairest in fruits; a crop
Life-giving, dense, its happy strength does yield.
Rich honies with green cane their fragrance join,
And milk flows potable in runnels full;
And with whate'er that sacred earth is green,
It all breathes life; and there Crete's healing gift
Is sweetly redolent. There, with smooth tide,
Flows in the placid plains a fount: four floods
Thence water parted lands. The garden robed
With flowers, I wot, keeps ever spring; no cold
Of wintry star varies the breeze; and earth,
After her birth-throes, with a kindlier blast
Repairs. Night there is none; the stars maintain
Their darkness; angers, envies, and dire greed
Are absent; and out-shut is fear, and cares

Driven from the threshold. Here the Evil One
Is homeless; he is into worthy courts
Out-gone, nor is't e'er granted him to touch
The glades forbidden. But here ancient faith
Rests in elect abode; and life here treads,
Joying in an eternal covenant;
And health without a care is gladsome here
In placid tilths, ever to live and be
Ever in light.
Here whosoe'er hath lived
Pious, and cultivant of equity
And goodness; who hath feared the thundering God
With mind sincere; with sacred duteousness
Tended his parents; and his other life
Spent ever crimeless; or who hath consoled
With faithful help a friend in indigence;
Succoured the over-toiling needy one,
As orphans' patron, and the poor man's aid;
Rescued the innocent, and succoured them
When prest with accusation; hath to guests
His ample table's pledges given; hath done
All things divinely; pious offices
Enjoined; done hurt to none; ne'er coveted
Another's: such as these, exulting all
In divine praises, and themselves at once
Exhorting, raise their voices to the stars;
Thanksgivings to the Lord in joyous wise
They psalming celebrate; and they shall go

Their harmless way with comrade messengers.

—TERTULLIAN,
"A Strain of the Judgment of the Lord"

———⚬⚬⚬———

Thomas à Kempis, 1380–1471, was an Augustinian monk and an exponent of the devotio moderna *movement, which encouraged liturgical reform in late-medieval Catholicism. His* The Imitation of Christ *remains one of the most popular books of spiritual guidance in the history of Western Christianity. It offers advice for cultivating a Christian life and preparing for future immortality. In the following passage, Kempis writes from the perspective of God and explains how the joys of heavenly life more than compensate for sufferings experienced in earthly life.*

Others shall be great in the praise of men, but about thee there shall be no word.

To others this or that shall be committed, but thou shalt be accounted a thing of no use.

At this nature will sometimes be troubled, and it is a great thing if thou bear it with silence.

In these and many such like things, the faithful servant of the Lord is wont to be tried, how far he can deny and break his will in all things.

There is scarcely anything wherein thou hast such need to die to thyself, as in seeing and suffering those things that are contrary to thy will; especially when that is commanded to be done, which seemeth unto thee inconvenient, or useless.

And because thou being under authority darest not resist the higher power, therefore it seems hard to thee to walk at another's beck, and to feel that thou must give up all thine own will.

But consider, my son, the fruit of these labors, the end near at hand, and the reward exceeding great; and thou wilt not grudge to bear them: rather thou wilt have the strongest comfort of thy patience.

For instead of that little of thy will, which now thou so readily forsakest, thou shalt always have thy will in heaven.

Yea, there thou shalt find all that thou canst wish, all that thou shalt be able to desire.

There thou shalt have within thy reach all good, without fear of losing it.

There shall thy will ever be one with me; it shall not covet any outward or selfish thing.

There none shall withstand thee, no man shall complain of thee, no man hinder thee, nothing come in thy way; but all things thou canst desire shall be there altogether present, and shall refresh thy whole affection, and fill it up to the brim.

There I will give thee glory for the reproach which here thou sufferedst, the garment of praise for heaviness, for the lowest place a kingly throne for ever.

There shall the fruit of obedience appear, the labor of repentance shall rejoice, and humble subjection shall be gloriously crowned.

—THOMAS À KEMPIS, *The Imitation of Christ*

The Book of Mormon *contains the revelations given to Joseph Smith in 1823. Mormonism is radically different from mainstream Christianity in many ways, but shares a belief in the divinity of Christ. The following passage from the* Book of Mormon *explains that, because physical resurrection cannot occur until after the second coming of Christ, the state of Paradise is granted to righteous souls between the time of death and the time of resurrection.*

Now, concerning the state of the soul between death and the resurrection—Behold, it has been made known unto me by an angel, that the spirits of all men, as soon as they are departed from this mortal body, yea, the spirits of all men, whether they be good or evil, are taken home to that God who gave them life.

And then it shall come to pass, that the spirits of those who are righteous are received into a state of happiness, which is called paradise, a state of rest, a state of peace, where they shall rest from all their troubles and from all care, and sorrow.

—Alma 40:11–12

⸻

Friedrich Nietzsche, 1844–1900, was a German philosopher whose harsh critique of the Christian religion of his day is contained in his book The Antichrist. *In the passage below, Nietzsche offers a new interpretation of the teachings of Christ, and a revision of traditional doctrines concerning the nature of the afterlife.*

If I understand anything of this great symbolist it is that he took for realities, for "truths", only *inner* realities—that he understood the rest, everything pertaining to nature, time, space, history, only as signs, as occasion for metaphor. The concept "the Son of Man" is not a concrete person belonging to history, anything at all individual or unique, but an "eternal" fact, a psychological symbol freed from the time concept. The same applies supremely to the *God* of this typical symbolist, to the "kingdom of God", to the "kingdom of Heaven", to "God's children". Nothing is more un-Christian than the *ecclesiastical crudities* of God as a *person*, of a "kingdom of God" which *comes*, of a "kingdom of Heaven" in the *Beyond*, of a "Son of God", the *second person* of the Trinity. . . .

The "kingdom of Heaven" is a condition of the heart—not something that comes "upon the earth" or "after death". The entire concept of natural death is *lacking* in the Gospel: death is not a bridge, not a transition, it is lacking because it belongs to quite another world, a merely apparent world useful only for the purpose of symbolism. The "hour of death" is *not* a Christian concept—the "hour", time, physical life and its crises, simply do not exist for the teacher of the "glad tidings".... The "kingdom of God" is not something one waits for; it has no yesterday or tomorrow, it does not come "in a thousand years"—it is an experience within a heart; it is everywhere, it is nowhere....

—FRIEDRICH NIETZSCHE, *The Antichrist*

JUDAISM

The Hebrew Bible in its literal reading contains only scattered references to the afterlife. It is probable that the Israelites during and prior to the biblical period concurred with many of the beliefs concerning the fate of the soul held by their neighbors, such as the Egyptians and the Babylonians, imagining an afterlife very much like earthly existence. Even today, many Jews dismiss the idea of an afterlife. In general, the emphasis of Judaism is on proper conduct in daily life, the establishment of social justice, and the practice of worship. Nevertheless, interpretations and mystical readings of the Scriptures have introduced certain key concepts about heaven into Judaism that have survived into the modern day and influenced the ideas of both Christianity and Islam.

The Garden of Eden is mentioned in Genesis as the original home of human beings; literary evidence from as early as 200 B.C.E. indicates that some Jews saw a return to the Garden of Eden, or Paradise, as the consequence of physical death. Other sources do not explicitly associate the "world to come" with Eden, but indicate that there is a place of peace and joy to which the dead travel. In addition to the concept of a "world to come," or Paradise, Judaism incorporates the notion of the physical resurrection of the dead, which occurs at the end of historical time. The resurrection of the dead is often linked to another event—the coming of the Messiah—though there is no necessary relationship between these events in Jewish eschatology. While the term "Messiah" originally referred to the historical king of Israel, it gradually came to mean a savior sent by God to restore the sovereignty of the Jewish people and usher in an era of peace and abundance. It is very difficult to distinguish descriptions of the messianic age from those of the Garden of Eden in many accounts. The picture of the afterlife in Judaism is further complicated by the ideas of the mystics, who suggested the possibility of reincarnation.

For the most part, the section which follows contains passages which describe a Paradise or a "world to come." This is because these descriptions emphasize the positive features of existence in the afterlife, and are most similar to the general notion of a "heaven" as understood in the West. The texts which follow share certain common features which are distinctive of the Jewish understanding of the afterlife. First, Paradise is not open only to Jews; because Jewish law is not incumbent upon non-Jews, non-Jews are judged according to the different standards God has set for them. All righteous people, who observe the laws God gave them particularly, may enter Paradise. Second, Paradise is not contrasted with an eternal hell; even in those sources which do identify Gehenna as a place of punishment, the suffering of sinners in Gehenna is not permanent. Gehenna exists as a place of purification; eventually, everyone is purified and is permitted to enter Paradise. Third, the study of the Torah and religious observance is generally believed to continue even in Paradise. This feature is not universal, however; some writers have suggested that many things which are prohibited in this world, such as the flesh of swine, are permitted in the next.

The final feature which unites all of the various Jewish eschatological ideas is freedom from oppression. Whether this freedom comes about at the end of time, through the agency of a Messiah, or in the repose of the dead, Jews have continually hoped that the persecution which has marked much of Jewish history will come to an end in the future.

The Babylonian Talmud, completed around 400 C.E., is the basic document of Jewish observance. Its voluminous contents include explanations of Jewish law and practice, interpretation of Scripture, ethical and spiritual tales, and speculations on everything from astronomy and meteorology to the fate of the soul after death. The following eight selections are all found in the Babylonian Talmud, and are identified by the particular section of the Talmud from which they are taken. The first five selections demonstrate the Rabbinic notion that the world to come may only be understood as the reversal of things taken for granted in this world.

R. Aha b. Hanina said: The world to come is not like this world. In this world, on hearing good tidings, a man says, "Blessed art thou who art good, and dispensest good"; and on hearing sad tidings he says, "Blessed art thou, the true Judge." But in the world to come he will only say, "Blessed art thou, who art good and dispensest good."

—Pesahim

It was a favourite saying of Rab: "Not like this world is the world to come." In the world to come there is neither eating nor drinking; no procreation of children or business transactions; no envy or hatred or rivalry; but the righteous sit enthroned, their crowns on their heads, and enjoy the lustre of the Shechinah.

—Berakhot

R. Johanan said: The Jerusalem of the world to come is unlike the Jerusalem of this world. The Jerusalem of this world all can enter who will; the Jerusalem of the world to come they only can enter who are appointed for it.

—Bava Batra

R. Joshua's son fell sick and swooned. His father asked him what he had seen. He replied, "I saw a topsy turvy world." R. Joshua said, "No, a purified world. How fares it with us Rabbis?" He said, "As we are honoured here, so we are honoured there. And I heard it said, 'Blessed is he who comes hither with his study fresh upon him.' Yet none can attain to the division of the martyrs."

—Bava Batra

As to Paradise, Resh Lakish said: If it is in the Land of Israel, its gate is Beth Shean; if it is in Arabia its gate is Beth Gerem; and if it is between the rivers, its gate is Damascus.

—Erubin

The Watch-House of the Sun

⁕

The next passage, also from the Babylonian Talmud, provides an elaborate description of seven heavens by Rabbi Judah. The passage illustrates that the Rabbis understood the heaven of human souls as only a small part of a vast metaphysical world beyond our own, including physical bodies like the sun, as well as spiritual entities like angels. The passage concludes with a warning against an excess of such cosmological speculation by Rabbi Aha b. Jacob.

Rabbi Judah said: There are two firmaments, for it is said: Behold, unto the Lord thy God belongeth heaven, and the heaven of heavens. Resh Lakish said: There are seven, namely, Vilon, Rakia, Shehakim, Zebul, Ma'on, Makon, and Arabot. Vilon serves no purpose except that it enters in the morning and goes forth in the evening, and renews each day the work of creation. Rakia is that in which sun and moon, stars and constellations are set. Shehakim is that in which millstones stand and grind manna for the righteous. Zebul is that in which the heavenly Jerusalem and the Temple and the Altar and built, and Michael, the great Prince, stands and offers up thereon an offering. Ma'on is that in which there are companies of Ministering Angels, who utter song by night and are silent by day for the sake of Israel's glory. Makon is that in which there are the stores of snow and stores of hail, and the loft of harmful dews and the loft of raindrops, the chamber of the whirlwind and storm, and the cave of vapour, and their doors are of fire. Arabot is that in which there are Right and Judgment and Righteousness, the treasures of life and the treasures of peace and the treasures of blessing, the souls of the righteous and the spirits and the souls which are yet to be born, and dew wherewith the Holy One, blessed be He, will hereafter revive the dead. There are, too, the Ofanim and the Seraphim, and the Holy Living Creatures, and the Ministering Angels, and the Throne of God; and the King, the Living God, high and exalted, dwells over them in Arabot. And darkness and thick cloud surround Him.

And Rabbi Aha b. Jacob said: There is still another Heaven above the heads of the living creatures, for it is written: And over the heads of the living creatures there was a likeness of a firmament, like the colour of the terrible ice, stretched forth over their heads above. Thus far you have permission to speak, thenceforward you have not permission to speak, for so it is written in the Book of Ben Sira: Seek not things that are too hard for thee, and search not out things that are hidden from thee. The things that have been permitted thee, think thereupon; thou hast no business with the things that are secret.

—Hagigah

The next two passages refer to the idea that at the end of time God will prepare a great banquet as a reward for those who were righteous *on earth. It is probable that this idea is more closely related to the tradition of the resurrection of the dead than to that of Paradise. Nevertheless, the passages have been included because they are some of the earliest sources of a prominent symbol for future reward used throughout Jewish writing. Leviathan, the main course of the first passage, is a mythical fish of enormous proportions.*

Rabbah said in the name of Rabbi Johanan: The Holy One, blessed be He, will in time to come make a banquet for the righteous from the flesh of Leviathan. The rest of Leviathan will be distributed and sold out in the markets of Jerusalem.

Rabbah in the name of Rabbi Johanan further stated: The Holy One, blessed be He, will in time to come make a tabernacle for the righteous of the skin of Leviathan. If a man is worthy, a tabernacle is made for him; if he is not worthy, a mere covering is made for him. If a man is worthy a covering is made for him; if he is not worthy a necklace is made for him. If a man is worthy a necklace is made for him; if he is not worthy an amulet is made for him. The rest of Leviathan will be spread by the Holy One, blessed be He, upon the walls of Jerusalem, and its splendour will shine from one end of the world to the other.

Resh Lakish said: The Holy One, blessed be He, will in time to come add to Jerusalem a thousand gardens, a thousand towers, a thousand palaces, and a thousand mansions; and each of these will be as big as Sepphoris in its prosperity.

—Bava Batra

Ulla Bira'ah said in the name of R. Eleazar: In the days to come the Holy One, blessed be He, will hold a chorus for the righteous and He will sit in their midst in the Garden of Eden and every one of them will point with his finger towards Him, as it is said, And it shall be said in that day: Lo, this is our God, for whom we waited, that He might save us; this is the Lord for whom we waited, we will be glad and rejoice in His salvation. (Isaiah 25:9)

—Ta'anith

The passage below, from a Rabbinic collection of scriptural interpretations, provides a beautiful example of exegesis in the Jewish tradition. Further, it offers an alternative interpretation of what life after death might signify.

God said to Moses, "Behold thy days draw near to die" (Deut. 31:14). Samuel bar Nahmani said: "Do days die? But it means that at the death of the righteous, their days cease from the world, yet they themselves abide, as it says, 'In whose hand is the soul of all the living' " (Job 12:10). Can this mean that the living alone are in God's hand, and not the dead? No, it means that the righteous even after their death may be called living, whereas the wicked, both in life and in death, may be called dead.

—Midrash Tanhuma

⊶⊷

The selection below is from the Midrash, *Rabbinic interpretations of passages from the Bible. It refers to the statement that God "breathed" His spirit into Adam found in Genesis. It extracts from the verse and the example of glass-blowing that human life is restored after death, and indicates that part of this restoration includes a reunion with loved ones.*

There was a man in Sepphoris whose son had died. A heretic sat by his side. R. Jose b. Halafta came to visit him. The heretic saw that he was smiling. He said to him, "Rabbi, why do you smile?" He replied, "I trust in the Lord of heaven that the man will see his son again in the world to come." Then that heretic said, "Is not his sorrow enough for the man that you should come and sadden him yet more? Can broken sherds be made to cleave again together? Is it not written, 'Thou shalt break them in pieces like a potter's vessel'?" (Ps. 2, 9).

Then R. Jose said, "Earthern vessels are made by water and perfected by fire; vessels of glass are both made by fire and perfected by fire; the former, if broken, cannot be repaired; the latter, if broken, can be repaired." The heretic said, "Why?" He replied, "Because they are made by blowing. If the glass vessel which is made by the blowing of a mortal man can be repaired, how much more the being who is made by the blessing of God."

—Bereshit Rabbah,
Rabbinic interpretations of Genesis

As mentioned in the introduction to this section, it is sometimes difficult to distinguish between individual life after death and the national rebirth ensuing upon the arrival of the Messiah. This passage conflates the world to come with the time of the Messiah, describing miraculous changes in human life commonly associated with heaven. Of note is the last sentence, which indicates that the world to come is not only the residence of the perfectly righteous, but even of those who have broken the commandments.

At some time in the days of the Messiah and in the world-to-come the righteous will have radiance of countenance. To what degree? There are some who will be given radiance of countenance such as the sun's when he goeth forth (Judg. 5:31) in the day's first hour before he attains the full might of his radiance. There are some who will be given radiance such as the sun's in the first two hours of the day; some, its radiance in the first three hours; some, its radiance in the first five hours; some its radiance in the first six hours. And some will be given radiance such as the sun's throughout the entire day. There are others who will be given radiance of countenance like the radiance of the moon at the time of the New Moon. Others will be given radiance such as the moon's on the fifth day in the month. Others such as the moon's on the tenth in the month. Others such as the moon's on the fifteenth day of the month. There are still others whose radiance will be like the great stars, and others like the small stars. There are still others who will be given the radiance of the firmament's atmosphere when it is clear of clouds. But there will be others, alas, whose faces will be as black as the bottom of a pot.

—Tanna debe Eliyyahu,
an early exegetical work

———

This selection, a medieval work concerning Paradise from a thirteenth-century text, is particularly concerned with the place of women in Paradise. It associates the various levels of Paradise with matriarchs, prophetesses, and other famous women in the Jewish tradition.

In Gan Eden, on the north side, are seven prepared realms and palaces for the righteous women in Israel who performed meritorious deeds for the Holy Blessed One by giving charity and from the merits of the Torah for their children. In the first realm will be found Batyah, the daughter of Pharaoh. How many will the righteous women be that are there? All those who reared orphans, showed kindness to scholars, showing the hospitality of their husbands, and giving charity secretly. Every day they are crowned with a shining crown of the splendor of the Shekhinah, and they proclaim over them, "Blessed are you who fortify and continue the growth of the branch of splendor in the world."

In the second realm there are many righteous women of Israel. There is Yokheved, the wife of Amram, who is chief over them. Three times a day they proclaim with respect to her: "Blessed are you that you have merited bearing a son whose head and feet stood among the thick cloud."

In the third realm there is Miriam the prophetess, with whom the righteous women stand. All those who encourage their husbands to walk in the good way and in the service of their Creator. In every realm, there are canopies of tranquility, and well-known angels have been appointed over every realm.

In the fourth realm is Hulda the prophetess and many pious women who reside in that division.

In the fifth realm there is Abigail, and with her are

many righteous women, dwelling in confidence, each in her own canopy.

From there on are those of the matriarchs: Sarah, Rebecca, Rachel, and Leah. At midnight when the Holy Blessed One enters with the righteous, a voice calls in the Garden: "You are righteous, prepare yourselves to meet your Maker! Blessed are you who have merited all this glory." At that time the souls will blossom forth and each of them will be paired together suitably and according to the realm of their works. They will see and attain their realm of their works. They will see and attain their realm with joy, "Eye has not seen, O God, except you." (Isaiah 64:3)

—Seder Gan Eden

This medieval account is in the genre of ascent literature, describing a mystical journey by Moses into the heavens. In the passage below Moses is informed by Metatron, the angelic Prince of the Divine Face, concerning the function of the first heaven, which seems to be the dispensation of Divine mercy and judgment into the world.

Moses went up to the first heaven, which corresponds to the first day of the week; there he saw streams upon streams of water. And he observed that this heaven was full of windows, and at each window stood an angel.

The Watch-House of the Sun

And Moses asked Metatron: "What are these windows?" And Metatron answered: "These windows are—the window of prayer, the window of request, the window of supplication, the window of crying tears, the window of joy, the window of satiation, the window of famine, the window of poverty, the window of riches, the window of war, the window of peace, the window of pregnancy, the window of birth, the window of the treasures of rain, the window of dew, the window of smallness, the window of greatness, the window of death, the window of life, the window of disease among men, the window of disease among animals, the window of healing, the window of sickness, the window of health." And Moses saw great things past finding out, "yea marvelous things without number." (Job 9:10)

—Gedulat Moshe, "The Greatness of Moses"

⸺⸺⸺⸻⸺⸺⸺

The following is a passage from pseudepigraphical work, written by an unknown author between the second century B.C.E. and the second century C.E. and attributed to Levi, the son of the biblical patriarch Jacob. It describes a series of levels within heaven which appear in similar form in other accounts of this type.

And I entered from the first heaven, and I saw there a great sea hanging. And further I saw a second heaven far brighter and more brilliant, for there was a boundless height also therein. And I said to the angel, Why is this so? And the angel said to me, Marvel not at this, for thou shalt see another heaven more brilliant and incomparable. And when thou hast ascended thither, thou shalt stand near the Lord, and shalt be His minister, and shalt declare His mysteries to men, and shalt proclaim concerning Him that shall redeem Israel. And by thee and Judah shall the Lord appear among men, saving every race of men. And from the Lord's portion shall be thy life, and He shall be thy field and vineyard, and fruits, gold, and silver. Hear, therefore, regarding the heavens which have been shown to thee. The lowest is for this cause gloomy unto thee, in that it beholds all the unrighteous deeds of men. And it has fire, snow, and ice made ready for the day of judgment, in the righteous judgment of God; for in it are all the spirits of the retributions for vengeance on men. And in the second are the hosts of the armies which are ordained for the day of judgment, to work vengeance on the spirits of deceit and of Beliar. And above them are the holy ones. And in the highest of all dwelleth the Great Glory, far above all holiness. In the heaven next to it are the archangels, who minister and make propitiation to the Lord for all the sins of ignorance of the righteous; offering to the Lord a sweet-smelling savour, a reasonable and a bloodless offering. And in the heaven below this are the angels who bear answers to the angels of the presence of the Lord. And in the heaven next to this are thrones and dominions, in which always they offer praise to God.

And thereupon the angel opened to me the gates of heaven, and I saw the holy temple, and upon a throne of glory the Most High. And He said to me: Levi, I have given thee the blessings of the priesthood until I come and sojourn in the midst of Israel.

—Testament of Levi

The Sefer ha-Bahir *is one of the primary texts of the Kabbalistic tradition, the set of Jewish mystical teachings which speculates on the process of Divine Creation, the nature of God, and the nature of the human soul. In the passage below, the* Bahir *explains that the purpose of creation was for God to bestow good, and that Eden may be understood both as the actual reward of humans after death and as a symbol for the Divine bestowal of good in general.*

The paradigm of gardens is Eden, and hence the question is posed, where is it and what is its spiritual significance?

The reply is that it is on earth. This indicates that the original Garden of Eden was physical, here on earth, and that it was not merely a spiritual entity.

In a conceptual sense, however, this has a deeper meaning. The concept of the Garden is in the conceptual

Earth, that is, in the Sefirah of Malkhut-Kingship, the last Heh of the Tetragrammaton.

The first three letters of the Tetragrammaton have already been discussed, and now it is the final Heh that must be explained. As stated earlier, it is the ultimate effect, the ultimate purpose of creation—"the final deed that was in the first thought."

God's purpose in creation was to bestow good and the place where this good is bestowed is in the Garden of Eden. It is for this reason that man's ultimate reward in the afterlife is called "Garden of Eden". Since God is the ultimate good, the good that He bestows is His own Essence. As discussed earlier, this is realized through Malkhut-Kingship.

—Sefer ha-Bahir

⸻

The selection from a medieval text excerpted below is interesting in its explanation of the dispensation of Divine reward. Those who serve God for a particular purpose attain that purpose. Only those who serve God purely out of love for him reach the highest state of closeness and union with Him.

The reward of an individual who serves God out of love consists in experiencing celestial joy of a wonderous character. I learned from my teacher, may he rest in peace, a clearer explanation concerning the rewards of those who devote themselves to God out of love. One who serves the King of the universe out of love, without expectation of reward in this world or the next—but out of love alone—will be compensated by the Holy One, blessed be He, Himself. If he serves Him for the sake of some earthly reward, for the purpose of acquiring wealth or having children, he receives his reward entirely in this world. Just as this world is transitory, so too is his reward. And if he serves God for the sake of securing a place in Paradise, his reward will be administered by the angels who tend there. But if he devotes himself to God out of pure love, his soul cleaves to the "Infinite One" as well as to His *Sefirot*, thereby uniting them in the proper manner.

Thus his reward from above is "to behold the graciousness of the Lord" [Ps. 27:4], as explained earlier in greater detail. For every person merits reward in the future in proportion to his earthly deeds. If he merits reward on the level of vital-soul alone, his resting place will be in the location where the vital-souls reside following death. And if he merits reward on the level of spirit, he will enjoy Paradise. If he merits reward on the level of super-soul, he will be privileged to ascend to the upper realm of Paradise. Those who attain the grade of super-soul are called God's lovers.

—ELIJAH DE VIDAS, *The Beginning of Wisdom*

The Watch-House of the Sun

—⟨∞⟩—

*Israel ben Eliezer Ba'al Shem Tov, c. 1700–1760, founded the
Jewish movement known as Hasidism. His teachings encouraged the
joyful worship of God and reinterpreted the observances of the Jewish
religion as mystical procedures which brought good into the world and
prepared for the coming of the Messiah. The following passage is taken
from a letter to his brother-in-law, Rabbi Abraham Gershon of
Kutow, and describes one of the Ba'al Shem Tov's own mystical
experiences. Because the souls of both the living and the dead are
found in the Garden of Eden, the letter challenges the notion that the
entrance of the soul into the Garden is an event which happens in
human time; rather, the soul moves through many worlds independent
of the constraints of time and space found in this world.*

For on the day of the New Year of the year 5507
(= September, 1746) I engaged in an ascent of the soul,
as you know I do, and I saw wondrous things in that
vision that I had never before seen since the day I had
attained to maturity. That which I saw and learned in
my ascent it is impossible to describe or to relate even
from mouth to mouth. But as I returned to the lower
Garden of Eden I saw many souls, both of the living and
the dead, those known to me and those unknown. They
were more than could be counted and they ran to and
fro from world to world through the path provided by
that column known to the adepts in the hidden science.
They were all in such a state of great rapture that the

mouth would be worn out if it attempted to describe it and the physical ear too indelicate to hear it. Many of the wicked repented of their sins and were pardoned, for it was a time of much grace. In my eyes, too, it was a great marvel that the repentance was accepted of so many whom you know. They also enjoyed great rapture and ascended, as mentioned above.

—ISRAEL BEN ELIEZER BA'AL SHEM TOV

Rabbi Joseph Karo, 1488–1575, was one of the greatest scholars of Jewish religious law; his Shulchan Aruch *remains for many Jews the basic source of guidance in religious practice. In addition to his great legal accomplishments, Karo was a mystic, who claimed to receive guidance from a spiritual voice, called a* maggid. *The following passage is excerpted from Karo's diary, and records the* maggid's *promise of future reward to Karo.*

And after all this I shall give you the merit of being burned for the sanctification of My name. All your sins and faults will be purged by fire so that you will rise from there like pure wool. All the saints in the Garden of Eden, the *Shekhinah* at their head, will come out to meet you, welcoming you with many songs and praises. They will lead you like a groom who walks in front and they will accompany you to your canopy. I have prepared for you seven canopies, one within the other, and seven canopies, one higher than the other. Within the innermost and highest of the canopies there will be seven rivers of fragrant balsam. It is all there ready for you. And there will be a golden throne with seven steps, embedded with numerous pearls and precious stones. All the saints will accompany you and sing before you until you arrive at the first canopy. There they will clothe you with a precious robe and so on at each canopy so that by the time you arrive at the final canopy you will be clothed with fourteen precious robes. Afterwards, two of the saints who accompany you will stand, one to the right and one to the left, like groomsmen for a groom, and they will help you to ascend the throne. As you ascend the throne they will put another robe on you in addition to the fourteen so that as you sit on the throne you will be wearing fifteen precious robes. They will take a crown hanging there and place it upon your head. There you will sit with one to the right of you and one to the left. All the saints will sit around you and you will discourse on the Torah. This will continue for one hundred and eighty days. . . . Afterwards, all the saints will arise to accompany you, with you in the front like a groom. They will walk behind you but some of them will go before you, proclaiming, "Pay homage to the son of the Holy, Supernal King. Pay homage to the image of the King." Thus they will sing until you arrive at the place where there are thirteen rivers of balsam. A garment will be removed from you as you immerse yourself in the first river and so on until thirteen garments will have been removed when you immerse yourself in the thirteenth river. Afterwards a river of fire will gush forth and as you immerse yourself in it the fourteenth robe will be removed. As you emerge a precious white robe will be made ready for you to wear and Michael the high priest will be ready to bring up your soul to the Holy One, blessed be He. From this stage onwards permission has not been granted to describe what will transpire. Eye has seen it not. . . .

—JOSEPH BEN EPHRAIM KARO,
Maggid Mesharim

ISLAM

*T*he Koran, unlike the Bible, provides numerous explicit descriptions of heaven within its text. These passages utilize profoundly physical and sensual language to describe the blessings which await those who follow the path of Islam. The recorded sayings and explanations of the Prophet Muhammad further confirm the Koranic revelations, and add to the details of the picture Muslims have of the future life of the righteous. The availability of canonical descriptions of heaven has served to create a uniformity in Muslim descriptions of the afterlife which is not present in either Judaism or Christianity.

The Muslim heaven is referred to in the Koran as a "Garden" or "Paradise." It is the habitation of beautiful maidens, known as *houris*, and beautiful youths, known as *wildan*, who were created exclusively to wait upon the desires of those souls reposing in Paradise. Paradise itself flows with rivers of honey, milk, and wine. In Paradise, Muslims are permitted to behold God in proportion to the degree of their worship and spiritual perfection. Paradise is eternal, and is juxtaposed with an eternal hell, the lurid details of which are also spelled out in the Koran.

The rewards of Paradise do not ensue immediately upon death in the Muslim tradition. Following death there is an intermediary phase, which lasts until the end of historical time, when the Day of Judgment arrives. On the Day of Judgment, God determines the fate of each individual soul based upon their activities in earthly life. Those who are privileged to enter Paradise or unfortunate enough to enter hell do so together; no soul is rewarded or punished for even an instant more than any other.

While there is a coherence to the various Muslim descriptions of heaven not found in other traditions, individual Muslim authors have emphasized certain features in accordance with their own understanding of the Koran and the words of the Prophet. This section contains selections both from the canonical religious works and the writings of various Muslim theologians and philosophers. Even within the seemingly clear description of the Koranic Paradise, numerous levels of interpretation may be found.

The following passages are all taken from the Koran, and are identified by the name of the chapter from which they were selected. The Koranic descriptions of Paradise use the language of the pleasures of ordinary life to give some hint of the joys awaiting the faithful. Endless abundance and eternal youth are basic elements of Paradise, in contrast to the scarcity and ephemerality which are characteristic of this world.

Announce to those who believe and do the things that are right, that for them are gardens 'neath which the rivers flow! So oft as they are fed therefrom with fruit for sustenance, they shall say, "This same was our sustenance of old." And they shall have its like given to them. Therein shall they have wives of perfect purity, and therein shall they abide for ever.

—The Cow

A picture of the Paradise which is promised to the God-fearing! Therein are rivers of water, which corrupt not: rivers of milk, whose taste changeth not: and rivers of wine, delicious to those who quaff it;

And rivers of honey clarified: and therein are all kinds of fruit for them from their Lord!

—Muhammad

From the evil therefore of that day hath God delivered them and cast on them brightness of face and joy;

And hath rewarded their constancy, with Paradise and silken robes:

Reclining therein on bridal couches, nought shall they know of sun or piercing cold:

Its shades shall be close over them, and low shall its fruits hang down:

And vessels of silver and goblets like flagons shall be borne round among them:

Flagons of silver whose measure themselves shall mete.

And there shall they be given to drink of the cup tempered with ginger

From the fount therein whose name is Selsebil.

Aye—blooming youths go round among them. When thou lookest at them thou wouldest deem them scattered pearls;

And when thou seest this, thou wilt see delights and a vast kingdom:

Their clothing green silk robes and rich brocade; with silver bracelets shall they be adorned; and drink of a pure beverage shall their Lord give them.

This shall be your recompense. You efforts shall meet with thanks.

—Man

But for those who dread the majesty of their Lord
shall be two gardens:
Which then of the bounties of your Lord will ye
twain deny?
With o'erbranching trees in each:
Which then of the bounties of your Lord will ye
twain deny?
In each two fountains flowing:
Which then of the bounties of your Lord will ye
twain deny?
In each two kinds of every fruit:
Which then of the bounties of your Lord will ye
twain deny?
On couches with linings of brocade shall they
recline, and the fruit of the two gardens
shall be within easy reach:
Which then of the bounties of your Lord will ye
twain deny?
Therein shall be damsels with retiring glances,
whom no man nor djinn hath touched
before them:
Which then of the bounties of your Lord will ye
twain deny?
Like jacynths and pearls:
Which then of the bounties of your Lord will ye
twain deny?
Shall the reward of good be aught but good?—

Which then of the bounties of your Lord will ye
twain deny?
And beside these shall be two other gardens:
Which then of the bounties of your Lord will ye
twain deny?
Of a dark green:
Which then of the bounties of your Lord will ye
twain deny?
With gushing fountains in each:
Which then of the bounties of your Lord will ye
twain deny?
In each fruits and the palm and the pomegranate:
Which then of the bounties of your Lord will ye
twain deny?
In each, the fair, the beauteous ones:
Which then of the bounties of your Lord will ye
twain deny?
With large dark eyeballs, kept close in their
pavilions:
Which then of the bounties of your Lord will ye
twain deny?
Whom man hath never touched, not any djinn:
Which then of the bounties of your Lord will ye
twain deny?
Their spouses on soft green cushions and on
beautiful carpets shall recline:
Which then of the bounties of your Lord will ye
twain deny?

Blessed be the name of thy Lord, full of majesty
and glory.

—The Merciful

These are they who shall be brought nigh to God,
In gardens of delight;
A crowd of the former
And few of the latter generations;
On inwrought couches
Reclining on them face to face:
Aye—blooming youths go round about to them
With goblets and ewers and a cup of flowing wine;
Their brows ache not from it, nor fails the sense:
And with such fruits as shall please them best,
And with flesh of such birds, as they shall long for:
And theirs shall be the Houris, with large dark eyes,
        like pearls hidden in their shells,
In recompense of their labours past.
No vain discourse shall they hear therein, nor charge
        of sin,
But only the cry, "Peace! Peace!"

—The Event

The following are sayings of the Prophet Muhammad, referred to as
hadith *in Arabic. In the first, the Prophet and founder of Islam*

explains that, unlike this world, Paradise is a place where people increase in health, strength, and beauty as time passes. The second describes in detail the experience of a soul arriving at Paradise.

Anas b. Malik reported that God's Messenger (may peace be upon him) said: In Paradise they will come to a street every Friday. The north wind will blow and will scatter fragrance on their faces and on their clothes. And they will increase in beauty and loveliness, and they will go back to their family with their beauty and loveliness increased, and their family will say to them: By God, you have been increased in beauty and loveliness since we saw you, and each will say: By God, you have been increased in beauty and loveliness since I saw you!

—from *Sahih Muslim*, a collection of the sayings of the Prophet

So they will reach the gate of the Garden, and its knocker is of red ruby. Then they will knock with it. The houris will receive them with plates in their hands. Each houri will go out to her master and embrace him and say: "You are my beloved. I am pleased with you and will love you forever," and she will enter the Garden with him.

There are seventy couches in the house. On each couch are seventy rugs. On each rug is a houri wearing seventy robes. The marrow of her legs is seen through the fineness of her robes. If one hair of the women of the people of the Garden were to fall to earth, it would give light to all the people of the earth.

—From a collection by Imam 'Abd ar-Rahim ibn Ahmad al-Qadi

───※───

The idea of Paradise pervades the Muslim culture. Not only theologians, but natural scientists and philosophers throughout the history of Islam have tried to explain its nature and form. Within the following selection, a Muslim philosopher explains the relationship between the spiritual world and the physical one.

They continued: The earth is made to thrive by its four great rivers, namely, the Tigris, the Euphrates, the Nile, and the Oxus; and every one of them has been given its own particular taste, differing from the tastes of the others. Furthermore, every single locality on earth has other small rivers special to it alone. Now the situation is the same in the celestial spheres. That is in them are the same number of great rivers, and they have different forms; and they also have smaller watercourses which reach to every region of them, so that every place is full of them. But that which flows in these rivers has no weight so as to seek the lowest level; rather, it has a form such that it can run through high places and low.

So it oscillates and surges up and down, like something travelling around in a circle.

They continued: The earth is surrounded by its seven great seas; and every one of them has qualities special to it alone. Furthermore, in every locality there are pools and marshes whose benefit redounds to the inhabitants of that locality. Now the situation is the same with the celestial sea. Indeed, the situation is also the same with the celestial mountains, and with the celestial winds. But the form of all these is untouched by corrosion, putrefaction, condensation, and turbidity. Also, as the earth is adorned with lofty edifices, exalted thrones, soaring staircases, and high chambers, and with elegant gardens, precious carpets, magnificent garments, and delicate vessels, so is the situation the same in that body in its natural disposition. And the rational soul which attains to perfect wisdom and devout service may in its spirituality become acquainted with all which that body contains, and then from there look upon these lower models with an eye which discriminates between sediment and purity, and between the effect and the cause. And this is the absolute happiness for human souls.

—AL-'AMIRI, *Kitab al-Amad 'ala l-Abad*

The following is a section from one of the classical expositions concerning Paradise. It adds details not present in the Koranic account, some derived from sayings of the Prophet and others from other sources. The discrimination between doers of different types of good deeds is noteworthy, as it emphasizes that Paradise is given as a reward for activity, not simply belief.

Ibn 'Abbas, may Allah be pleased with him, said: The Gardens have eight gates of gold inlaid with jewels. Written on the first gate is "There is no God except God, Muhammad is the messenger of God." It is the gate of the prophets, messengers, martyrs and the generous.

The second gate is the gate of those who prayed, who were excellent in ritual washing and the basic elements of the prayer.

The third gate is that of those who gave Zakat cheerfully.

The fourth gate is that of those who commanded good and forbade the reprehensible.

The fifth gate is the gate of those who rooted out their appetites and prevented passions.

The sixth gate is the gate of those who did Hajj and 'Umra.

The seventh gate is the gate of those who fought Jihad.

The eighth gate is the gate of those who turned their eyes from forbidden things and did good actions of respect to parents, relatives, and others.

There are eight Gardens. The first is the Abode of Majesty, and it is of white pearl.

The second is the Abode of Peace, and it is of red ruby.

The third is the Abode of Shelter, and it is of green chrysolite.

The fourth is the Garden of Immortality, and it is of red and yellow coral.

The fifth is the Garden of Bliss, and it is of white silver.

The sixth is the Garden of Firdaws, and it is of red gold.

The seventh is the Garden of 'Aden, and it is of white pearl.

The eighth is the Abode of Rest, and it is of red gold, and it is the dome of the Gardens, and it is raised over the Gardens. It has two gates, and the two leaves are of gold and silver. Between each of the two leaves is what is between heaven and earth. It is built of gold and silver bricks. Its mud is musk and its earth is amber and its straw is saffron. Its castles are of pearl and its rooms are of ruby. Its doors are of jewels, and in it are rivers. There is the River of Mercy which flows in all the Gardens, and its pebbles are pearls, with a white brighter than snow, and it is sweeter than honey. In it is the River of Abundance, and it is the river of our Prophet Muhammad, peace be upon him. Its trees are pearls and rubies. In it is the River of Camphor and the River of

Water Coming From Above, and the River of Ease of Swallowing and the River of Sealed Nectar. Beyond that are rivers whose numbers are not known.

—*Kitab Ahwal al-Qiyama*

⊷⊶⊷

Al-Ghazālī, 1058–1111, was the greatest systematic theologian of Islam. He wrote on many aspects of Muslim life, from the practice of rituals to ethics to philosophy and mysticism. In the following passage, Al-Ghazālī expands upon a topic found among the sayings of the Prophet, and presents a beautiful image of the Day of Judgment immediately prior to the opening of Paradise to the righteous.

In the *Sahih* it says that the first thing God decides concerns cases of bloodshed, and the first to be given their recompense, are those who have lost their vision. On the day of resurrection God calls to the blind and says to them, "You are the most appropriate, that is, the most worthy to look at Us." Then He gives them life and says to them, "Go to my right." A white banner is awarded to them and put in the hand of Shu'ayb, who goes in front of them. With them are angels of light, whose number only God can calculate, conducting them in solemn procession as one would lead a bride; they pass on with them to the Sirat with the speed of light-ning. Each of them is characterized by patience, forbearance and knowledge, as were Ibn Abbas and those like him in this community.

Then the call comes, "Where are the people of affliction? He wants those who have infirmities!" So they are brought and God revivifies them with a salutation in the sweetest of tongues; then He orders them to His right. To them is given a green banner, put in the hand of Job, and he goes before them on the right. Those who have suffered are characterized by patience, forbearance and knowledge, as were 'Aqil ibn Abi Talib, and those like him in this community.

Then comes the call, "Where are the people of righteousness?" They are brought to God and He welcomes them, saying what He wishes to say. Then He orders them to His right; a red banner is given to them, put in the hand of Joseph, who goes in front of them on the right. The righteous are characterized by patience, forbearance and knowledge, as were Rashid ibn Sulayman and those like him in this community.

Then comes the call, "Where are those who love God?" They are brought to God and He welcomes them, saying what He wishes to say. Then he orders them to His right; a yellow banner is given them, placed in the hand of Aaron, and he goes before them on the right. Those who love God are characterized by patience and knowledge and forbearance, never annoyed or displeased with any earthly circumstances, as were Abu Turab (by

whom I mean 'Ali ibn Abi Talib) and those like him in
this community.

Then the call comes, "Where are those who weep
out of fear of God?" They are brought to God, and their
tears when weighed against the blood of the martyrs and
the ink of the learned tip the balance. So He orders them
to His right; a multi-colored banner is given them, because they wept for different reasons—one cried out of
fear, another out of desire and a third in remorse. The
banner is put in the hand of Noah.

—AL-GHAZĀLĪ,
Kitab al-Durra al-Fakhira fi Kashf 'Ulum al-Akhira

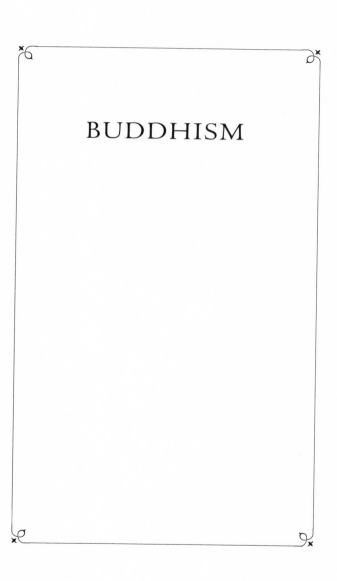

BUDDHISM

*G*autama Siddhārtha, known throughout the world as the Buddha, the "Enlightened One," lived from approximately 560–480 B.C.E. His recorded sermons, as well as the explanations and teachings of other religious teachers, form an enormous canon of Buddhist religious texts. The Buddhist tradition is not unified; in many cases the teachings of the Buddha were combined with cultural and religious ideas from local areas, giving Chinese Buddhism, for example, a very different cast than South Indian Buddhism.

This tremendous diversity within the Buddhist tradition is one reason why descriptions of heaven may be found in Buddhism at all. A reading of the teachings of the Buddha alone would suggest that the question of an afterlife is almost irrelevant to the essential message of Buddhism. The religion teaches that the only absolute end to suffering lies in the extinction of desires; disappointment and frustration are the inevitable consequence of desire. As long as humans create emotional attachments to the world they will suffer, as the things they love pass away. The goal is to see the world as it is, ephemeral and illusory, without forming bonds or attachments to it. In keeping with this idea, many Buddhists have seen heaven as simply one more temptation, one more desire, preventing the mind from achieving freedom and causing it to hope for a relief which will not actually come.

Despite this aspect of the Buddhist worldview, local Buddhist traditions and individual Buddhists have done a great deal of speculating as to the possibility of a life of total bliss. Some have conjectured that just as this world is a place of perpetual pain and frustration, there may be a world which is perpetual joy and fulfillment. Others have wondered what the state of liberation itself is like, and seen in it a paradisiacal existence similar to the concept of heaven found in other traditions. No matter what their reasons, Buddhists have written about the possibility of states of infinite happiness, and some of their texts are collected on the following pages. It is important to remember in reading this chapter that the object in Buddhism is liberation; while a heaven may exist, it too must be transcended.

The following passage is taken from a sutra, a recorded sermon of the Buddha. In it the Buddha explains to his disciple, Malunkyaputta, why he has not spoken at length about the afterlife. The Buddha teaches that whether or not there is a heaven, the goal of religion should be the same: to seek clarity of mind and freedom from attachments.

Then the venerable Malunkyaputta arose at eventide from his seclusion, and drew near to where the Blessed One was; and having drawn near and greeted the Blessed One, he sat down respectfully at one side. And seated respectfully at one side, the venerable Malunkyaputta spoke to the Blessed One as follows: "Reverend Sir, it happened to me, as I was just now in seclusion and plunged in meditation, that a consideration presented itself to my mind, as follows: 'These theories which the Blessed One has left unelucidated, has set aside and rejected—the world is eternal, that the world is not eternal, ...that the saint neither exists nor does not exist after death—these the Blessed One does not elucidate to me. I will draw near to the Blessed One and inquire of him concerning this matter. If the Blessed One will elucidate them to me, in that case will I lead the religious life under the Blessed One. If the Blessed One will not elucidate them, I will abandon religious training and return to the lower life of a layman.'"

"The religious life, Malunkyaputta, does not depend on the dogma that the world is eternal, nor on the dogma that the world is not eternal. Whether the dogma obtain, Malunkyaputta, that the world is eternal, or that the world is not eternal, there still remain birth, old age, death, sorrow, lamentation, misery, grief, and despair, for the extinction of which in the present life I am prescribing. Accordingly, Malunkyaputta, bear always in mind what it is that I have not elucidated, and what it is that I have elucidated. And what, Malunkyaputta, have I not elucidated? I have not elucidated, Malunkyaputta, that the world is eternal; I have not elucidated that the world is not eternal. . . . I have not elucidated that the saint neither exists nor does not exist after death. And why, Malunkyaputta, have I not elucidated this? Because, Malunkyaputta, this profits not, nor has to do with the fundamentals of religion, nor tends to aversion, absence of passion, cessation, quiescence, the supernatural faculties, supreme wisdom, and Nirvana; therefore have I not elucidated it. And what, Malunkyaputta, have I elucidated? Misery, Malunkyaputta, have I elucidated; the origin of misery have I elucidated; the cessation of misery have I elucidated; and the path leading to the cessation of misery have I elucidated. And why, Malunkyaputta, have I elucidated this? Because, Malunkyaputta, this does profit, has to do with the fundamentals of religion, and tends to aversion, absence of passion, cessation, quiescence, knowledge, supreme wisdom, and Nirvana;

therefore have I elucidated it. Accordingly, Malunkyaputta, bear always in mind what it is that I have not
elucidated, and what it is that I have elucidated."

—Sutras

———⟨∞⟩———

*The Tibetan Book of the Dead has become famous in the
West for its intriguing account of the experience of the soul in the
days which immediately follow bodily death. This excerpt describes
one of the many episodes on the journey between death and reincarnation or liberation: a state of peace and comfort like heaven, which—
although it feels safe—is an obstacle to true liberation.*

O son of noble family, after being unconscious for
four and a half days you will move on, and awakening
from your faint you will wonder what has happened to
you, so recognise it as the bardo state. At that time,
samsara is reversed, and everything you see appears as
lights and images.

The whole of space will shine with a blue light, and
Blessed Vairocana will appear before you from the central
Realm, All-pervading Circle. His body is white in colour,
he sits on a lion throne, holding an eight-spoked wheel
in his hand and embracing his consort the Queen of
Vajra Space. The blue light of the skandha of consciousness in its basic purity, the wisdom of the *dharmadhatu,*

luminous, clear, sharp and brilliant, will come towards you from the heart of Vairocana and his consort, and pierce you so that your eyes cannot bear it. At the same time, together with it, the soft white light of the gods will also come towards you and pierce you. At that time, under the influence of bad karma, you will be terrified and escape from the wisdom of the *dharmadhatu* with its bright blue light, but you will feel an emotion of pleasure towards the soft white light of the gods. At that moment do not be frightened or bewildered by the luminous, brilliant, very sharp and clear blue light of supreme wisdom, for it is the light-ray of the buddha, which is called the wisdom of the *dharmadhatu*. Be drawn to it with faith and devotion, and supplicate it, thinking, "It is the light-ray of the Blessed Vairocana's compassion, I take refuge in it." It is Blessed Vairocana coming to invite you in the dangerous pathway of the bardo; it is the light-ray of Vairocana's compassion.

Do not take pleasure in the soft white light of the gods, do not be attracted to it or yearn for it. If you are attracted to it you will wander into the realm of the gods and circle among the six kinds of existence. It is an obstacle blocking the path of liberation, so do not look at it, but feel longing for the bright blue light.

—*The Tibetan Book of the Dead*

━━◦◦◦━━

Sukhavati is a blessed world described in certain Buddhist scriptures which is in many ways the opposite of this world; where in this world desires usually go unfulfilled, in Sukhavati every desire is always fulfilled. Sukhavati is not necessarily the place to which dead souls travel; it is an independent and distinct world. The text from which this description is taken, The Larger Sukhavati-vyuha, *is intended to illustrate the point that no matter whether the problem is too little fulfillment or too much fulfillment, the task must be to release oneself from all types of attachment.*

And, O Ananda, the world called Sukhavati belonging to that Lord Amitabha is prosperous, rich, good to live in, fertile, lovely, and filled with many gods and men. Then, O Ananda, in that world there are neither hells, nor the brute creation, nor the realm of departed spirits, nor bodies of Asuras, nor untimely births. And there do not appear in this world such gems as are known in the world Sukhavati.

Now, O Ananda, that world Sukhavati is fragrant with several sweet-smelling scents, rich in manifold flowers and fruits, adorned with gem trees, and frequented by tribes of manifold sweet-voiced birds, which have been made by the Tathagata. And, O Ananda, those gem trees are of several colours, of many colours, and of many hundred thousand colours. There are gem trees there of golden colour, and made of gold. There are those of

silver colour, and made of silver. There are those of
beryl colour, and made of beryl. There are those of crystal colour, and made of crystal. There are those of
coral colour, and made of coral. There are those of red
pearl colour, and made of red pearls. There are those of
diamond colour, and made of diamonds.

There are some trees of two gems, gold and silver. There are some of three gems, gold, silver, and beryl.
There are some of four gems, gold, silver, beryl, and
crystal. There are some of five gems, gold, silver,
beryl, crystal, and coral. There are some of six gems, gold,
silver, beryl, crystal, coral, and red pearls. There are some
of seven gems, gold, silver, beryl, crystal, coral, red pearls,
and diamonds as the seventh.

And, O Ananda, the roots, trunks, branches, small
branches, leaves, flowers, and fruits of all those trees are
pleasant to touch, and fragrant. And, when those trees
are moved by the wind, a sweet and delightful sound
proceeds from them, never tiring and never disagreeable
to hear. That Buddha country, O Ananda, is always on
every side surrounded by such trees made of the seven
gems, by masses of banana trees, and rows of palm trees
made of the seven gems, and entirely surrounded with
golden nets, and wholly covered with lotus flowers, made
of all kinds of gems.

And if, after they are satisfied, the inhabitants of that
world wish different kinds of perfumes, then with these
very heavenly kinds of perfumes the whole Buddha coun-

try is scented. And whosoever wishes to perceive there such perfume, every perfume of every scent of the Gandharvaraga does always reach his nose.

And in the same manner, if they desire musical instruments, banners, flags, umbrellas, cloaks, powders, ointments, garlands, and scents, then the whole Buddha country shines with such things. If they desire cloaks of different colours and many hundred thousand colours, then with these very best cloaks the whole Buddha country shines. And the people feel themselves covered with them.

And if they desire such ornaments, as for instance, head-ornaments, ear-ornaments, neck-ornaments, hand- and foot-ornaments, namely, diadems, earrings, bracelets, armlets, necklaces, chains, ear-jewels, seals, gold strings, girdles, gold nets, pearl nets, jewel nets, nets of bells made of gold and jewels, then they see that Buddha country shining with such ornaments adorned with many hundred thousand jewels, that are fastened to ornament trees. And they perceive themselves to be adorned with these ornaments.

— *The Larger Sukhavati-vyuha*

The following is a Thai Buddhist description of a blessed world of the gods, similar in many respects to Sukhavati. In this heavenly

*world, however, though things have enormous proportions and endure
for astonishing lengths of time, they eventually, just as in the physical
world, fade away and perish.*

Indra then goes to play at one of the parks where
he enjoys himself a great deal. Sometimes Indra dis-
mounts from the elephant Eravana, and goes on foot to
play. The heavenly path is 40,000 wa wide and there are
a great number of beautiful female attendants who wear
all kinds of superb ornaments. Thus they go to play in
the pleasure park.

On the outside, near the stone slab at the Paricchattaka tree, there is a large pavilion called the Sudhamma-sabha pavilion. It measures 2,400,000 wa across
and the same on the opposite side; it is 4,000,000 wa
high and the distance around it is 7,200,000 wa. The
floor of the pavilion is made of gem crystal and is decorated with the seven kinds of gems; and a golden wall
surrounds the pavilion. There is a kind of flower called
asavati that is very fragrant; and even though it takes as
long as 1,000 years for the flowers to bloom, the devata
love them, wish to admire them, and wish to wear them
behind their ears. Because they love these flowers, the
devata, when they see that the buds of these flowers are
ready to bloom, take turns staying and watching the buds,
even though they have to wait for the entire thousand
years. Even though the flowers of the coral tree called
Paricchattaka take a 100 years to bloom, the devata still

have a great love and desire for them; if they look and see that these flowers are going to bloom, the devata take turns staying and watching the flowers until they do bloom. When the flowers are in full bloom on every twig and branch, they emit rays that are bright and very beautiful; in fact, the rays of these Paricchattaka flowers glow for a distance of 800,000 wa. The devata never at any time stop climbing to get these flowers. When any devata wants to obtain these flowers he takes pieces of cloth to wrap them in or a container to put them in, and a wind blows the flowers so that they fall into the place that is ready for them. When the devata are not ready to receive them, a wind blows and supports the flowers in the air so that they will not fall to the ground. There is a certain kind of wind that carefully blows the flowers into the Sudhamma-sabha pavilion, and there is a kind of wind that carefully blows them into rows, just as if someone had neatly strung them. When the flowers have withered, a wind carefully blows the flowers out and away from the Sudhamma pavilion.

—*Three Worlds According to King Ruang*

HINDUISM

*T*he Hindu tradition is one of the oldest on the Earth; throughout its history it has gone through tremendous evolution and has been the birthplace of a wide range of philosophies and practices. Hinduism is perhaps best known in the West for its notion of reincarnation, the idea that the soul passes from one life to the next, remaining the same in its essence but taking on an endless succession of forms. In the Hindu system of reincarnation, as generally understood, there is very little place for heaven: No one experiences eternal death, so there is no need for a place of eternal reward.

Hinduism, however, has absorbed through its history a number of regional traditions that have different views about the nature of life and death.

The earliest Hindu texts, the Vedas, speak of a "Realm of the Dead," and name Yama as the deity responsible for overseeing the welfare of departed spirits. Other texts explain that it is possible to escape the cycle of birth and rebirth, and dwell in a place of endless repose. Still other texts conjecture heavens and hells which are impermanent, temporary places of joy or misery, stages in the larger process of reincarnation. Indeed, in some of these heavens, the joy is spoiled by the omnipresent awareness that it will one day disappear. In many cases, the heavens described are associated with astronomical bodies, such as the moon or the stars.

In Hinduism, the soul may take the form of plants, animals, or even stones. For Hindus who believe in the idea of a heaven, it is theoretically possibly even for a soul which began its journey as sand by the sea or as a wild animal to reach its bliss. The process of self-perfection, which may lead to heaven, extends over many lifetimes. It is a gradual fulfillment of the debts and obligations known as *karma* across a timescale which transcends individual human awareness.

The following selection is from an esoteric text of the school of thought known as Vedanta, *which posits the existence of an eternal, unchanging soul identical with the Essence of God. It describes the journey to heaven briefly, with an emphasis on the stages of the journey.*

When the person goes away from this world he comes to the wind. Then the wind makes room for him, like the hole of a carriage wheel, and through it he mounts higher. He comes to the sun. Then the sun makes room for him, like the hole of a Lambara, and through it he mounts higher. He comes to the moon. Then the moon makes room for him, like the hole of a drum, and through it he mounts higher, and arrives at the world where there is no sorrow, no snow. There he dwells eternal years.

—Upanisads

This passage is from the Bhagavad Gita, the sixth book of the Hindu national epic the Mahabharata. *The speaker, Krishna, equates heaven with the stars, and explains that those who do good deeds are permitted to sit there. Nevertheless, the hierarchical nature of this world, as well as the absence of permanent fulfillment, are also characteristics of heaven.*

Learn from me now the seats in which creatures going up dwell, and which I shall describe truly. Hearing this, you will learn the highest knowledge, and decision regarding action. All the worlds in the forms of stars, and this lunar sphere, and also this solar sphere which shines in the world by its own lustre, know these to be the seats of men who perform meritorious actions. All these, verily, fall down again and again in consequence of the exhaustion of their actions. And there, too, in heaven, there are differences of low, high, and middling. Nor, even there, is there satisfaction, even after a sight of most magnificent splendour. Thus have I stated to you these seats distinctly.

—Bhagavad Gita

The following passage from a priestly text is a general explanation of the later Hindu concept of heaven. It is only one of many stages in the process of reincarnation, and its inhabitants are not free from fear and misery over the thought of their possible descent from heaven.

A man repeatedly goes through a cycle of births and deaths. In this way, he rolls like a clock on the wheel of the world. Sometimes a man attains heaven, sometimes he goes to hell and sometimes a dead man reaps both heaven and hell. And sometimes born again in this earth he reaps the fruits of his own acts. And sometimes enjoying the fruits of his own acts within a short time he breathes his last. Sometimes, O best of Brahmanas, living in heaven or hell for a short time on account of his limited merit or demerit he is born in this earth. O father, the dwellers of heaven are seen by them to enjoy happiness—and then those, brought down to perdition, think that there is a great misery in hell. Even in heaven there is incomparable misery, for from the time of ascension every one conceives in his mind, "I shall fall." Beholding the people of hell, they attain to might misery thinking day and night, "I shall be brought to this condition."

—Markandeya Purana

━━━

This is one of the most explicit descriptions of heaven in the Hindu tradition. It is taken from the Garuda Purana Saroddhara, *which treats both heaven and hell equally. The features which make heaven most satisfying in this account are its absence of extremes, and the unchanging condition of satisfaction which embraces its inhabitants.*

The Blessed Lord said: Listen, O Tarksya, I will tell you about that shining city of Justice, which is accessible to Narada and others and is reached by the very meritorious.

Between the south and southwest is the city of the son of Vivaswata, all built of diamonds, resplendent, impregnable by Holy Ones or Demons.

It is declared to be four-angled, with four gateways, surrounded by high ramparts and measuring a thousand yojanas.

In that city is the very lovely dwelling of Chitragupta, which extends to the number of twenty-five yojanas,

Surrounded with shining ramparts of iron, up to ten heights, with hundreds of streets decorated with flags and banners,

Abounding in chariots, resounding with songs and music, decorated by skillful painters and constructed by divine architects,

Beautiful with gardens and parks, and sounding with the songs of various birds; habited in every part by celestial damsels and choristers.

Chitragupta, seated on his most wonderful throne in that assembly, considers the lives of men individually.

He is never mistaken in distinguishing between good and evil deeds, or by whom good or evil deeds have been done.

Chitragupta records the good and evil of men. Twenty yojanas before the abode of Chitragupta,

The Watch-House of the Sun

In the middle of the city, is the very resplendent mansion of the king of justice. It is shining with jewels, and splendid like lightning, flame, and the sun.

It is certainly two hundred yojanas in extent, and measures fifty yojanas in height.

It is supported by thousands of pillars, decorated with emeralds, ornamented with gold, and is full of palaces and mansions,

Pleasing to the mind with cupolas of the splendour of the autumnal sky; with beautiful crystal stairways and walls beautified with diamonds.

And with windows of strings of pearls, decorated with flags and banners; rich with the sound of bells and drums; and embellished with golden fringes,

Filled with various wonders; with hundreds of golden doors; beautiful with trees, plants and creepers without thorns.

With these and other embellishments decorated always—it was created by the architect of the Universe by the power of his own Yoga.

In that there is a divine assembly place which is a thousand yojanas in extent, splendid like the sun, full of light, and in every way satisfying.

With no extreme heat and no extreme cold; most ravishing to the mind with no sorrows and no old age there, and no trouble of hunger and thirst.

All there are in a condition of happiness, whether

they be human or divine; the eatables are tasteful and plentiful, and enjoyable in every way.

The water, both hot and cold, is sweet; the sounds and other things there are pleasant; and trees always bear the fruit desired.

That assembly, O Tarksya, has no bondage, is enchanting, is a fulfiller of desires, and was created by the Architect of the Universe by doing meditations for a long time.

—*Garuda Purana Saroddhara*

⚬⚬⚬

This passage is a selection from a funerary hymn which addresses the soul of the deceased individual. It instructs him concerning the proper route of travel and behavior in the Realm of the Dead. Yama, the King of the Dead, was the first mortal to die. He is responsible for the care of human souls in the afterlife.

Go forth, go forth on those ancient paths on which our ancient fathers passed beyond. There you shall see the two kings, Yama and Varuna, rejoicing in the sacrificial drink.

Unite with the fathers, with Yama, with the rewards of your sacrifices and good deeds, in the highest heaven. Leaving behind all imperfections, go back home again, merge with a glorious body.

Run on the right path, past the two brindled, four-eyed dogs, the sons of Sarama, and then approach the fathers, who are easy to reach and who rejoice at the same feast as Yama.

Yama, give him over to your two guardian dogs, the four-eyed keepers of the path, who watch over men. O king, grant him happiness and health.

The two dark messengers of Yama with flaring nostrils wander among men, thirsting for the breath of life. Let them give back to us a life of happiness here and today, so that we may see the sun.

—Rig Veda

The following passage is from an esoteric text of the Vedanta tradition. It explains that the Self is eternal and unchanging, though it appears to change as it enters various forms. The last four paragraphs refer to those who are able to realize the unchanging and eternal Self within them; they are exempt from the process of reincarnation and enjoy endless, perfect bliss.

Well then, O Gautama, I shall tell thee this mystery, the old Brahman, and what happens to the Self, after reaching death.

Some enter the womb in order to have a body, as

organic beings, others go into inorganic matter, according to their work and according to their knowledge.

He, the highest Person, who is awake in us while we are asleep, shaping one lovely sight after another, that indeed is the Bright, that is Brahman, that alone is called the Immortal. All worlds are contained in it, and no one goes beyond. This is that.

As the one fire, after it has entered the world, though one, becomes different according to whatever it burns, thus the one Self within all things becomes different, according to whatever it enters, and exists also without.

As the one air, after it has entered the world, though one, becomes different according to whatever it enters, thus the one Self within all things becomes different, according to whatever it enters, and exists also without.

As the sun, the eye of the whole world, is not contaminated by the external impurities seen by the eyes, thus the one Self within all things is never contaminated by the misery of the world, being himself without.

There is one ruler, the Self within all things, who makes the one form manifold. The wise who perceive him within their Self, to them belongs eternal happiness, not to others.

There is one eternal thinker, thinking non-eternal thoughts, who, though one, fulfils the desires of many. The wise who perceive him within their Self, to them belongs eternal peace, not to others.

They perceive that highest indescribable pleasure,

saying, "This is that. How then can I understand it? Has it its own light, or does it reflect light?"

The sun does not shine there, nor the moon and the stars, nor these lightnings, and much less this fire. When he shines, everything shines after him; by his light all this is lighted.

—Katha-Upanishad

ZOROASTRIANISM

The ancient Persian religion of Zoroastrianism is named for the prophet Zarathushtra, or Zoroaster, who taught that the cosmos was held in tension by two absolute, Divine forces, one good and one evil. Human beings are central in that they are neutral, and by their good and evil choices can determine the fate of the whole universe. While Zoroastrianism in the modern day claims only a handful of adherents, throughout history it has had a powerful influence on other religions of the world. For example, many scholars of religion attribute the Western concept of angels, as well as the idea of a personified Devil, to Zoroastrianism.

Heaven is an integral part of the worldview of Zoroastrianism. It is the place of eternal reward for those who have observed the ritual requirements of the religion. These rituals place an emphasis on purity, familial harmony, and the proper treatment of animals. The ideology behind these rituals constructs righteousness as a triad: good thoughts, good words, and good deeds. Each one follows from the one before it, so the cultivation of goodness must begin with developing the proper beliefs and the appropriate religious mind-set.

The heaven of Zoroastrianism is explicitly described in the texts attributed to Zarathushtra himself, as well as later works. A host of characters are met in these descriptions, and the soul's interactions with them form some of the liveliest and most interesting reading among the world's religious scriptures. The texts in the following chapter rely on the imagery of this world to communicate their vision of the world of endless peace and happiness which awaits those who observe the religion taught by Zarathushtra. Also noteworthy are the descriptions of the journey toward heaven, which are exemplary of the larger concept of the spiritual world in Zoroastrianism.

This text, part of the canon of Zoroastrianism, summarizes the features of heaven considered most desirable in Zoroastrianism: freedom from want, fear, and harm, and the bestowal of pleasure by the angels which inhabit heaven. The text also suggests that the reward of those who merit heaven is proportional to the good deeds they have done.

How are the nature of heaven and the comfort and pleasure which are in heaven? The reply is this, that it is lofty, exalted, and supreme, most brilliant, most fragrant, and most pure, most supplied with beautiful existences, most desirable, and most good, and the place and abode of the sacred beings. And in it are comfort, pleasure, joy, happiness, and welfare, more and better even than the greatest and supremest welfare and pleasure in the world; and there is no want, pain, distress, or discomfort whatsoever in it; and its pleasures and the welfare of the angels are from that constantly beneficial place, the full and undiminishable space, the good and boundless world. And the freedom of the heavenly from danger from evil in heaven is like unto their freedom from disturbance, and the coming of the good angels is like unto the heavenly ones' own good works provided. This prosperity and welfare of the spiritual existence is more than that of the world, as much as that which is unlimited and everlasting is more than that which is limited and demoniacal.

—Zend Avesta

❦

The Book of Arda Viraf *is a lengthy compendium on the nature of both heaven and hell, as well as a summary of the various rites which are to be performed at a funeral. The selection below distinguishes rewards based upon the occupations the deceased had in life. The special regard given to agriculturalists and shepherds, for example, shows how important these occupations were in Zoroastrian life.*

I came to a place, and I saw the souls of several people who remain in the same position. And I asked the victorious Srosh, the pious, and Ataro, the angel, thus: "Who are they? and why remain they here?"

Srosh, the pious, and Ataro, the angel, said thus: "They call this place Hamestagan; and these souls remain in this place till the future body; and they are the souls of those men whose good works and sin were equal. Speak out to the worlds thus: 'Let not avarice and vexation prevent you from doing a very easy good work; for everyone whose good works are three bits more than his sin, goes to heaven; they whose sin is more, go to hell; they in whom both are equal, remain among these Hamestagan till the future body.' Their punishment is cold, or heat, from the revolution of the atmosphere; and they have no other adversity."

And afterwards, I put forth the first footstep to the star track, on Humat, the place where good thoughts are received with hospitality. And I saw those souls of the pious whose radiance, which ever increased, was glittering as the stars; and their throne and seat were under the radiance, and splendid and full of glory.

When I put forth the second footstep, it was to Hukht of the moon track, the place where good words find hospitality; and I saw a great assembly of the pious.

When I put forth the third footstep on Huvarsht, there where good deeds are received with hospitality, there I arrived. There is the radiance which they call the highest of the highest; and I saw the pious on thrones and carpets made of gold; and they were people whose brightness was like unto the brightness of the sun.

I put the fourth footstep unto the radiance of Gar-odman, the all-glorious; and the souls of the departed came to meet us, and they asked a blessing, and offered praise, and they spoke thus: "How hast thou come forth, O pious one? From that perishable and very evil world, thou hast come unto this imperishable, unmolested world. Therefore taste immortality, for here you see plea-sure eternally."

I also saw the souls of warriors, whose walk was in the supremest pleasure and joyfulness, and together with that of kings; and the well-made arms and equipments of those heroes, were made of gold, studded with jewels, well-ornamented and all embroidered; and they were in wonderful trousers, with much pomp and power and tri-umph. And it seemed to me sublime.

I also saw the souls of agriculturists, in a splendid

place, and glorious and thick majestic clothing; as they stood, and offered praise, before the spirits of water and earth, trees and cattle; and they utter thanksgiving and praise and benediction; their throne is also great, and the place they occupy is good. And it seemed to me sublime.

I saw also the souls of artisans who, in the world, served their rulers and chieftains; as they sat on thrones which were well-carpeted and great, splendid and embellished. And it seemed to me very sublime.

I also saw the souls of shepherds, by whom, in the world, quadrupeds and sheep were employed and fed, and preserved from the wolf and thief and tyrannical man. And at appointed times, water and grass and food were given; and they were preserved from severe cold and heat; and the males were allowed access at the usual time, and properly restrained when inopportune; whereby very great advantage, profit and benefit, food and clothing were afforded to the men of that time. Which souls walked among those who are brilliant, on a beautiful eminence, in great pleasure and joy. And it seemed to me very sublime.

I also saw the souls of the faithful, the teachers and inquirers, in the greatest gladness on a splendid throne. And it seemed to me sublime.

I also saw the friendly souls of interceders and peace-seekers, who ever increased thereby their brilliance, which was like the stars and moon and sun; and they ever walked agreeably in the light of the atmosphere.

I also saw the pre-eminent world of the pious, which is the all-glorious light of space, much perfumed with sweet basil, all-bedecked, all-admired, and splendid, full of glory and every joy and every pleasure, with which no one is satiated.

—*The Book of Arda Viraf*

In this passage, the god of absolute Good, Ahura Mazda, directly answers a question Zarathushtra has asked about the afterlife. It emphasizes the journey toward heaven made by the departed soul. The beautiful maiden, Vohumano, and the Amesha-Spentas are all characters which recur in Zoroastrian descriptions of heaven.

O Maker of the material world, thou Holy One! Where are the rewards given? Where does the rewarding take place? Where is the rewarding fulfilled? Whereto do men come to take the reward that, during their life in the material world, they have won for their souls? Ahura Mazda answered: "When the man is dead, when his time is over, then the wicked, evil-doing Daevas cut off his eyesight. On the third night, when the dawn appears and brightens up, when Mithra, the god with beautiful weapons, reaches the all-happy mountains, and the sun is rising: Then the fiend, named Vizaresha, O Spitama

Zarathushtra, carries off in bonds the souls of the wicked Daeva-worshippers who live in sin. The soul enters the way made by Time, and open both to the wicked and to the righteous. At the head of the Chinvad bridge, the holy bridge made by Mazda, they ask for their spirits and souls the reward for the worldly goods which they gave away here below. Then comes the beautiful, well-shapen, strong and well-formed maid, with the dogs at her sides, one who can distinguish, who has many children, happy, and of high understanding. She makes the soul of the righteous one go up above the Haraberezaiti; above the Chinvad bridge she places it in the presence of the heavenly gods themselves. Up rises Vohumano from his golden seat; Vohumano exclaims: 'How hast thou come to us, thou holy one, from that decaying world into this undecaying one?' Gladly pass the souls of the righteous to the golden seat of Ahura Mazda, to the golden seat of the Amesha-Spentas, to the Garonmanem, the abode of Ahura Mazda, the abode of the Amesha-Spentas, the abode of all the other holy beings."

—Zend Avesta

This beautiful passage records a dialogue between the departed soul and a beautiful, spiritual maiden, who is revealed to be the conscience of the departed person. According to Zoroastrian tradition, the actions of the good person in life beautify his or her conscience in the spiritual world.

At the end of the third night, when the dawn appears, it seems to the soul of the faithful one as if it were brought amidst plants and scents, it seems as if a wind were blowing from the region of the south, a sweet-scented wind, sweeter-scented than any other wind in the world. And it seems to him as if his own conscience were advancing to him in that wind, in the shape of a maiden fair, bright, white-armed, strong, tall-formed, high-standing, thick-breasted, beautiful of body, noble, of a glorious seed, of the size of a maid in her fifteenth year, as fair as the fairest things in the world. And the soul of the faithful one addresses her, asking: "What maid art thou, who art the fairest maid I have ever seen?" And she, being his own conscience, answers him: "O thou youth of good thoughts, good words, and good deeds, of good religion, I am thy own conscience! Everybody did love thee for that greatness, goodness, fairness, sweet-scentedness, victorious strength and freedom from sorrow, in which thou didst appear to me; and so thou, O youth of good thoughts, good words, and good deeds, of good religion! didst love me for that greatness, goodness, fairness, sweet-scentedness, victorious strength, and freedom from sorrow, in which I appear to thee. When thou wouldst see a man making derision and deeds of idolatry, or rejecting the poor and shutting his door, then thou wouldst sit singing the Gathas and worshipping the good waters and Atar, the son of Ahura Mazda, and rejoicing the faithful that would come from near or from afar. I was lovely and thou madest me still lovelier; I was fair and thou madest me still fairer; I was desirable and thou madest me still more desirable; I was sitting at a forward place and thou madest me sit in the foremost place, through this good thought, through this good speech, through this good deed of thine; and so henceforth men worship me for my having long sacrificed unto and conversed with Ahura Mazda." The first step that the soul of the faithful man made, placed him in the good-thought paradise; the second step that the soul of the faithful man made, placed him in the good-word paradise; the third step that the soul of the faithful man made, placed him in the good-deed paradise; the fourth step that the soul of the faithful man made, placed him in the endless lights.

—Zend Avesta

BAHĀ'I

*T*he Bahā'i religion is one of the most recent traditions to surface in the world. It was founded in Iran by Mirza Hoseyn Ali Nuri, 1817–1892, who called himself the Bahaullah or Bahā' Allāh. The Bahāullāh was martyred in the city of Acre at the hands of Ottoman authorities. His teachings, based on personal spiritual revelations, emphasized the unity underlying all religions, and the sameness of the God named by every religious tradition.

The Bahā'i descriptions of heaven are set in the magnificent and beautiful language which characterizes all of the Bahāullāh's work. The Bahāullāh emphasizes the ineffability and splendor of the experience of heaven, as well as the great longing felt by each soul for the experience of heaven. The Bahá'í heaven is a place where human beings dwell with their Lord and experience an indescribable closeness and unity with Him.

In the following passage, the Baháʼulláh explains that language is inadequate to describe the blessings of heaven. Nothing that has ever existed can equal its marvels, and nothing is comparable to it.

O Nasir, O My servant! God, the Eternal Truth, beareth Me witness. The Celestial Youth hath, in this Day, raised above the heads of men the glorious Chalice of Immortality, and is standing expectant upon His seat, wondering what eye will recognize His glory, and what arm will, unhesitatingly, be stretched forth to seize the Cup from His snow-white Hand and drain it. Only a few have as yet quaffed from this peerless, this soft-flowing grace of the Ancient King. These occupy the loftiest mansions of Paradise, and are firmly established upon the seats of authority. By the righteousness of God! Neither the mirrors of His glory, nor the revealers of His names, nor any created thing, that hath been or will ever be, can ever excel them, if ye be of them that comprehend this truth. O Nasir! The excellence of this Day is immensely exalted above the comprehension of men, however extensive their knowledge, however profound their understanding. How much more must it transcend the imaginations of them that have strayed from its light, and been shut out from its glory! Shouldst thou rend asunder the grievous veil that blindeth thy vision, thou wouldst behold such a bounty as naught, from the beginning that hath no beginning till the end that hath no end, can either resemble or equal. What language should He Who is the Mouthpiece of God choose to speak, so that they who are shut out as by a veil from Him can recognize His glory? The righteous, inmates of the Kingdom on high, shall drink deep from the Wine of Holiness, in My name, the all-glorious. None other besides them will share such benefits.

—BAHĀULLĀH

In this passage, the Bahāullāh provides more details as to some of the blessings to be found in heaven. The argument given at the end of the passage is compelling: If there is no heaven, why should religious people throughout history have suffered such persecution to attain it?

And now concerning thy question regarding the soul of man and its survival after death. Know thou of a truth that the soul, after its separation from the body, will continue to progress until it attaineth the presence of God, in a state and condition which neither the revolution of ages and centuries, nor the changes and chances of this world, can alter. It will endure as long as the Kingdom of God, his sovereignty, His dominion and power will endure. It will manifest the signs of God and His attributes, and will reveal His loving kindness and bounty. The movement of My Pen is stilled when it attempteth to befittingly describe the loftiness and glory of so exalted a station. The honor with which the Hand of Mercy will invest the soul is such as no tongue can adequately reveal, nor any other earthly agency describe. The Maids of Heaven, inmates of the loftiest mansions, will circle around it, and the Prophets of God and His chosen ones will seek its companionship. With them that soul will freely converse, and will recount unto them that which it hath been made to endure in the path of God, the Lord of all worlds. If any man be told that which hath been ordained for such a soul in the worlds of God, the Lord of the throne on high and of earth below, his whole being will instantly blaze out in his great longing to attain that most exalted, that sanctified and resplendent station. . . . The world beyond is as different from this world as this world is different from that of the child while still in the womb of its mother. Even the materialists have testified in their writings to the wisdom of these divinely appointed Messengers, and have regarded the references made by the Prophets to Paradise, to hell fire, to future reward and punishment, to have been actuated by a desire to educate and uplift the souls of men. Consider, therefore, how the generality of mankind, whatever their beliefs or theories, have recognized the excellence, and admitted the superiority, of these Prophets of God. These Gems of Detachment are acclaimed by some as the embodiments of wisdom, while others believe them to be the mouthpiece of God Himself. How could such Souls have consented to surrender themselves unto their enemies if they believed all the worlds of God to have been reduced to this earthly life? Would they have willingly suffered such afflictions and torments as no man hath ever experienced or witnessed?

—BAHÁULLÁH

THE ANCIENT

WORLD

*T*his chapter contains a number of passages from the cultures of the ancient Mediterranean world, including the Egyptian, Greek, Roman, and ancient Levantine traditions. The contents of this section are widely varied, and express a number of different insights about the nature of the afterlife. The ideas contained in these passages have been influential in the development of the Jewish and Christian concepts of heaven; indeed, even the concept of a soul found in these traditions may be seen as an extension of ancient Mediterranean ideas. These texts, which originated in polytheistic traditions lacking the idea of an omnipotent God, form an interesting comparison to those originating in monotheistic cultures. Ancient Mediterranean religions often attribute to the human soul a degree of power and autonomy without parallel in Judaism and Christianity.

The ancient Mediterranean cultures shared a popular belief in the physical existence of the body in a heavenly underworld or a sky-heaven, complete with the need to eat, drink, and sleep. Some cultures, such as the Egyptian, made great efforts to prepare souls for existence in this life through practices such as mummification, or filling the grave with provisions for the next world. These practices survived in various forms even in the Greek and Roman worlds, where coins were placed on the eyes to pay the fare of the Boatman of the Underworld, who conducted the souls of the departed to their graves. Because of the relatively intact nature of the soul, communication with the dead was considered possible, and was frequently utilized.

Within this popular context, mystery cults and philosophical movements developed their own more spiritualized concepts of heaven. Some of the passages from these groups are included as well, to illustrate the complexity and sophistication found in the concepts of heaven of the ancient world.

This Egyptian passage enumerates some of the powers and favors afforded to the dead in the afterlife. The Ba *was the spiritual representation of the physical body which travelled into the afterlife. As long as the body was preserved, Egyptians believed that the* Ba *would continue its existence in heaven.*

Thou shalt come in and go out, thy heart rejoicing, in the favour of the Lord of the Gods, a good burial [being thine] after a venerable old age, when age has come, thou assuming thy place in the coffin, and joining earth on the high ground of the west. Thou shalt change into a living Ba and surely he will have the power to obtain bread and water and air; and thou shalt take shape as a heron or swallow, as a falcon or a bittern, whichever thou pleasest. Thou shalt cross in the ferryboat and shalt not turn back, thou shalt sail on the waters of the flood, and thy life shall start afresh. Thy Ba shall not depart from thy corpse and thy Ba shall become divine with the blessed dead. The perfect Bas shall speak to thee, and thou shalt be an equal amongst them in receiving what is given on earth. Thou shalt have power over water, shalt inhale air, and shalt be surfeited with the desires of thy heart. Thine eyes shall be given to thee so as to see, and thine ears so as to hear, thy mouth speaking and thy feet walking. Thy arms and thy shoulders shall move for thee, thy flesh shall be firm, thy muscles shall be easy and thou shalt exult in all thy limbs. Thou shalt examine thy body and find it whole and sound, no ill whatever adhering to thee. Thine own true heart shall be with thee, yea, thou shalt have thy former heart. Thou shalt go up to the sky, and shalt penetrate the Netherworld in all forms that thou likes.

—Coffin Texts, derived from tomb hieroglyphics

∞

This passage is one example of descriptions of spiritual journeys to the afterworld which are extant in ancient Mediterranean texts. In this particular formulation of the journey, enormous hardships and selectivity form obstacles to the attainment of a peaceful afterlife.

The way which we must take is long and has no end. Parasangs are not measured on it, and it is not marked by milestones. Torturers are left behind on it, watch-house keepers and toll-keepers sit on it. The chains are forged and held in readiness, the irons are polished and set at hand; the cauldrons, which guard the souls of the wicked, simmer. On the road is an ocean which has no passage. Each one is brought to it and conveyed across by his own donations and alms-giving. His works precede him as his messenger. The way which we must take is crammed with thistles and thorns. Seven walls encircle it, and mountains in which there is no gap. The scales are set up there and from one thousand they choose one soul that is good and enlightened. . . .

—*Books of the Songs of the Dead*

⟨∞⟩

This lengthy poetic description of a journey to the afterlife details a number of spiritual stations which must be passed before the soul can continue to its rest. The passage is obtained by virtue of the good works the soul performed in life. The state of bliss itself is associated with radiance, bliss, and union with the source of life.

I fly and proceed thither, until I reach the watch-house
    of the sun,
I cry: "Who will guide me past the watch-house of the
    sun?"
"Your reward, your good works, your alms, and your
    goodness will guide you past the watch-house of the
    sun."
How greatly I rejoice, how greatly my heart rejoices.
How much I look forward to the day when my struggle
    is over, to the day when my struggle is over and my
    course is set towards the Place of Life.
I hasten and proceed thither, until I reach the watch-
    house of the moon, I cry: "Who will guide me past
    the watch-house of the moon?"
"Your reward, your good works, your alms, and your

goodness will guide you past the watch-house of the moon."

How greatly I rejoice, how greatly my heart rejoices.

I hasten and proceed thither, until I reach the watch-house of fire, I cry: "Who will guide me past the watch-house of fire?"

"Your reward, your good works, your alms, and your goodness will guide you past the watch-house of fire."

How greatly I rejoice, how greatly my heart rejoices.

I hasten and proceed thither, until I reach the watch-house of the Seven, I cry: "Who will guide me past the watch-house of the Seven?"

"Your reward, your good works, your alms, and your goodness will guide you past the watch-house of the Seven."

How greatly I rejoice, how greatly my heart rejoices.

I hasten and proceed thither, until I reach the watch-house of Ruha, I cry: "Who will guide me past the watch-house of Ruha?"

"Your reward, your good works, your alms, and your goodness will guide you past the watch-house of Ruha."

How greatly I rejoice, how greatly my heart rejoices.

I hasten and proceed thither, until I reach the water-brooks.

When I arrived at the water-brooks, a discharge of radiance met me.

It took me by the palm of my right hand and brought
me over the streams.
Radiance was brought and I was clothed in it, light was
brought and I was wrapped in it.
The Life supported the Life.
The Life found Its Own.
Its Own did the Life find, and my soul found that for
which it yearned.

—*Books of the Songs of the Dead*

The Book of Enoch *is one of the most influential works in the
development of Jewish and Christian concepts of heaven. It tells the
story of one of the earliest descendents of the biblical Adam, Enoch,
who was lifted up into heaven and shown the nature of God, the
universe, and the afterlife. In this selection, Enoch sees the abode of
the righteous, as well as the four archangels who inhabit heaven.*

I saw the habitations and couches of the saints.
There my eyes beheld their habitations with the angels,
and their couches with the holy ones. They were entreat-
ing, supplicating, and praying for the sons of men; while
righteousness like water flowed before them, and mercy
like dew was scattered over the earth. And thus shall it
be with them for ever and for ever. At that time my eyes
beheld the dwelling of the elect, of truth, faith, and right-

eousness. Countless shall be the number of the holy and the elect, in the presence of God for ever and for ever. Their residence I beheld under the wings of the Lord of spirits. All the holy and the elect sung before him, in appearance like a blaze of fire; their mouths being full of blessings, and their lips glorifying the name of the Lord of spirits. And righteousness incessantly dwelt before them. There was I desirous of remaining, and my soul longed for that habitation. There was my antecedent inheritance; for thus had I prevailed before the Lord of spirits.

After this I beheld thousands of thousands, and myriads of myriads, and an infinite number of people, standing before the Lord of spirits. On the four wings likewise of the Lord of spirits, on the four sides, I perceived others, besides those who were standing before him. Their names, too, I know; because the angel, who proceeded with me, declared them to me, discovering to me every secret thing. Then I heard the voices of those upon the four sides magnifying the Lord of glory. The first voice blessed the Lord of spirits for ever and for ever. The second voice I heard blessing the elect One, and the elect who suffer on account of the Lord of spirits. The third voice I heard petitioning and praying for those who dwell upon earth, and supplicate the name of the Lord of spirits. The fourth voice I heard expelling the impious angels, and prohibiting them from entering into the presence of the Lord of spirits, to prefer accusations against the inhabitants of the earth. After this I besought the angel of peace, who proceeded with me, to explain all that was concealed. I said to him, Who are those whom I have seen on the four sides, and whose words I have heard and written down? He replied, The first is the merciful, the patient, the holy Michael. The second is he who presides over every suffering and every affliction of the sons of men, the holy Raphael. The third, who presides over all that is powerful, is Gabriel. And the fourth, who presides over repentance, and the hope of those who will inherit eternal life, is Phanuel. These are the four angels of the most high God and their four voices, which at that time I heard.

—*Book of Enoch*

⸻

The Poimandres *is one of the most important sections of the* Corpus Hermeticum, *the texts attributed to the mystical teacher Hermes Trismegistus. This passage describes the division of the soul into its elemental parts: each part returns to the source of its origin. The eighth part of the soul, its most divine portion, returns to a blessed existence in the presence of its Creator.*

To this Poimandres said: When thy material body is to be dissolved, first thou surrenderest the body by itself unto the work of change, and thus the form thou hadst doth vanish, and thou surrenderest thy way of life, void of its energy, unto the Daimon. The body's senses next pass back into their sources, becoming separate, and resurrect as energies; and passion and desire withdraw into that nature which is void of reason. And thus it is that man doth speed his way thereafter upwards through the Harmony. To the first zone he gives the Energy of Growth and Waning; unto the second [zone], Device of Evils [now] de-energized; unto the third, the Guile of the Desires de-energized; unto the fourth, his Domineering Arrogance, [also] de-energized; unto the fifth, unholy Daring and the Rashness of Audacity, de-energized; unto the sixth, Striving for Wealth by evil means, deprived of its aggrandizement; and to the seventh zone, Ensnaring Falsehood, de-energized. And then, with all the energizings of the Harmony stript from him, clothed in his proper Power, he cometh to that Nature which belongs unto the Eighth, and there with those-that-are hymneth the Father. They who are there welcome his coming there with joy; and he, made like to them that sojourn there, doth further hear the Powers who are above the Nature that belongs unto the Eighth, singing their songs of praise to God in a language of their own. And then they, in a band, go to the Father home; of their own selves they make surrender of themselves to Powers, and [thus] becoming Powers they are in God. This [is] the good end for those who have gained Gnosis—to be made one with God.

—*Poimandres*

The following two selections are taken from the Orphic Gold Plates: tiny, engraved gold tablets which were placed with the dead who were initiated into the ancient Greek mysteries of Orpheus. The Plates contained instructions for the soul to use on its journey to the afterlife.

Thou shalt find to the left of the House of Hades a spring, And by the side thereof standing a white cypress. To this spring approach not near. But thou shalt find another, from the Lake of Memory, cold water flowing forth, and there are guardians before it. Say, "I am a child of Earth and starry Heaven; but my race is of Heaven (alone). This ye know yourselves. But I am parched with thirst and I perish. Give me quickly the cold water flowing forth from the Lake of Memory." And of themselves they will give thee to drink of the holy spring, And thereafter among the other heroes thou shalt have lordship.

—Orphic Gold Plate

But as soon as the spirit hath left the light of the sun, go to the right as far as one should go, being right wary in all things. Hail, thou who hast suffered the suffering. This thou hadst never suffered before. Thou art become god from man. A kid thou art fallen into milk. Hail, hail to thee journeying the right hand road, by holy meadows and groves of Persephone.

—Orphic Gold Plate

The "Myth of Er" recounted in this passage from Plato tells of a soldier who died and came back to life. He is able to describe firsthand the events of the journey to the afterlife, and the nature of heaven.

"Indeed, I have no 'mighty long tale of Alcinoos' to tell you," said I, "but the tale of a mighty man, Er, son of Armenios, a Pamphyllian by nation. He met his end in battle once upon a time; and when the dead were taken up after ten days, the bodies already decayed, he was found whole; taken home and about to be buried on the twelfth day, while he lay on the pyre, he came to life again, and alive again he told what he had seen in the other world. When his soul went forth, he said, it travelled with many others, until they reached a wonderful region, in which were

two openings in the earth side by side, and two others in the heaven above facing them. Between these
judges were seated. These gave judgment, and, according to the judgment, they commanded the just men to
proceed to the right and upwards through heaven, after hanging on the breasts of the judged ones a token
to show the judgment; the unjust they sent down to
the left, these also having tokens hanging behind of
all they had done. When he himself approached they
told him he must become a messenger to mankind of
things there, and they commanded him to hear and
see everything in the place. So here he watched the
souls departing by two of the openings of heaven and
earth when sentence had been passed on them, and,
by the other two, souls returning, those coming up
out of one in the earth covered with dirt and dust,
others coming out of the other down from heaven
pure and clean. The souls which arrived from time to
time appeared to have come from a long journey, and
were glad to come out into the meadow; there they
encamped as at a fair, and any that were acquainted
greeted each other; the souls that came out of the
earth asked the others news of their part, and the
souls from heaven asked those what befell in their
place. They recounted their histories to each other;
those, weeping and lamenting when they recalled what
they had suffered and seen in their sojourn under-

ground—the sojourn, they said, lasted a thousand years; on the other hand, the souls out of heaven told of bliss and sights incredibly beautiful."

—PLATO, *The Republic*

———

Pindar's Olympian Odes *were written to commemorate the victors of events in the Olympic Games. The selection below, from the second "Ode," refers to the peace and pleasure popularly associated with the afterworld.*

O'er the Good soft suns the while
Through the mild day, the night serene,
Alike with cloudless lustre smile,
Tempering all the tranquil scene.
Theirs is leisure; vex not they
Stubborn soil or watery way,
To wring from toil want's worthless bread:
No ills they know, no tears they shed,
But with the glorious Gods below
Ages of peace contented share.
Meanwhile the Bad with bitterest woe
Eye-startling tasks, and endless tortures wear.

All whose stedfast virtue thrice
Each side the grave unchanged hath stood

The Watch-House of the Sun

Still unseduced, unstain'd with vice,
They by Jove's mysterious road
Pass to Saturn's realm of rest,
Happy isle that holds the blest;
Where sea-born breezes gently blow
O'er blooms of gold that round them glow,
Which Nature boon from stream or strand
Or goodly tree profusely pours;
Whence pluck they many a fragrant band,
And braid their locks with never-fading flowers.

—PINDAR, "Second Olympian Ode"

NATIVE

TRADITIONS

*T*his final chapter contains a variety of accounts of heaven from the religions of indigenous traditions from various parts of the world. Though this sampling is by no means representative of the diversity of ideas regarding heaven, a few selections have been provided for contrast and comparison with the writings from the great religions of the world. In many cases, the ideas about heaven seen in Christianity, Judaism, Islam, Zoroastrianism, and even the Eastern and ancient religions share remarkable similarities due to centuries of mutual influence. The indigenous traditions included here did not have contact for the most part with these larger religious traditions, and in them can be seen fresh and unusual perspectives on heaven.

In many cases, indigenous traditions do not make the same distinctions between the physical and spiritual worlds that are present in the great religions. The realms of the living and the dead are seamlessly interconnected. Communication with the dead is often taken for granted, and the afterlife bears a great resemblance to this life in many instances. Heaven is not always a place of bliss, either; sometimes, it is simply a *different* place, a different world where the laws of life and nature are altered in surprising and peculiar ways.

The absence of textual samples from most indigenous traditions makes collecting descriptions of heaven very difficult. For the most part, the selections which follow are records of oral traditions, or retellings of traditional stories.

The Thompson River Tribes of Canada have a concept of a parallel world of the spirits where life is recognizable, but changed in unusual ways. The world is pleasant and carefree: Singing and dancing are the norm, and men and women mix freely, with their needs comfortably met.

The country of the souls is underneath us, toward the sunset; the trail leads through a dim twilight. Tracks of the people who last went over it, and of their dogs, are visible. The path winds along until it meets another road which is a shortcut used by the shamans when trying to intercept a departed soul. The trail now becomes much straighter and smoother, and is painted red with ochre. After a while it winds to the westward, descends a long gentle slope, and terminates at a wide shallow stream of very clear water. This is spanned by a long slender log, on which the tracks of the souls may be seen. After crossing, the traveller finds himself again on the trail, which now ascends to a height heaped with an immense pile of clothes—the belongings which the souls have brought from the land of the living and which they must leave here. From this point the trail is level, and gradually grows lighter. Three guardians are stationed along this road, one on either side of the river and the third at the end of the path; it is their duty to send back those souls whose time has not yet come to enter the land of the dead. Some souls pass the first two of these, only to be turned back by the third, who is their chief and is an orator who sometimes sends messages to the living by the returning souls. All of these men are very old, gray-headed, wise, and venerable. At the end of the trail is a great lodge, mound-like in form, with doors at the eastern and the western sides, and with a double row of fires extending through it. When the deceased friends of a person expect his soul to arrive, they assemble here and talk about his death. As the deceased reaches the entrance, he hears people on the other side talking, laughing, singing, and beating drums. Some stand at the door to welcome him and call his name. On entering, a wide country of diversified aspect spreads out before him. There is a sweet smell of flowers and an abundance of grass, and all around are berry bushes laden with ripe fruit. The air is pleasant and still, and it is always light and warm. More than half the people are dancing and singing to the accompaniment of drums. All are naked but do not seem to notice it. The people are delighted to see the newcomer, take him up on their shoulders, run around with him, and make a great noise.

—An oral tradition of the
Thompson River Tribes

———

This Winnebago ritual instruction is addressed to the soul of the deceased. It provides detailed instructions for the behavior of the soul on its journey to heaven. The deceased is exhorted to intercede on behalf of his still-living relatives. The memory of the soul's earthly life is taken away, so that longing for the former life does not blemish the enjoyment of heaven.

I suppose you are not far away, that indeed you are right behind me. Here is the tobacco and here is the pipe which you must keep in front of you as you go along. Here also are the fire and the food which your relatives have prepared for your journey. In the morning when the sun rises you are to start. You will not have gone very far before you come to a wide road. That is the road you must take. As you go along you will notice something on your road. Take your war club and strike it and throw it behind you. Then go on without looking back. As you go farther you will again come across some obstacle. Strike it and throw it behind you and do not look back. Farther on you will come across some animals, and these also must you strike and throw behind you. Then go on and do not look back. The objects you throw behind you will come to those relatives whom you have left behind you on earth. They will represent victory in war, riches, and animals for food. When you have gone but a short distance from the last place where you threw the objects behind, you will come to a round lodge and there you will find an old woman. She is the one who is to give you further information. She will ask you, "Grandson, what is your name?" This you must tell her.

Then you must say, "Grandmother, when I was about to
start from the earth I was given the following objects
with which I was to act as mediator between your and
the human beings." Then you must put the stem of the
pipe in the old woman's mouth and say, "Grandmother,
I have made all my relatives lonesome, my parents, my
brothers, and all the others. I would therefore like to
have them obtain victory in war, and honours. That was
my desire as I left them downhearted upon the earth. I
would that they could have all that life which I left
behind me on earth. This is what they asked. This, likewise, they asked me, that they should not have to travel
on this road for some time to come. They also asked to
be blessed with those things that people are accustomed
to have on earth. All this they wanted me to ask of you
when I started from the earth. They told me to follow
the four steps that would be imprinted with blue marks,
Grandmother." "Well, Grandson, you are young but you
are wise. It is good. I will now boil some food for you."
Thus she will speak to you and then put a kettle on the
fire and boil some rice for you. If you eat it you will
have a headache. Then she will say, "Grandson, you have
a headache, let me cup it for you." Then she will break
open your skull and take out your brains and you will
forget all about your people on earth and where you came
from. You will not worry about your relatives. You will
become like a holy spirit. Your thoughts will not go as

far as earth, as there will be nothing carnal about you. Now the rice that the old woman will boil will really be lice. For that reason you will be finished with everything evil. Then you will go on stepping in the four footsteps mentioned before and that were imprinted with blue earth. You are to take the four steps because the road will fork there. All your relatives who died before you will be there. As you journey on you will come to a fire running across the earth from one end to the other. There will be a bridge across it but it will be difficult to cross because it is continually swinging. However, you will be able to cross it safely, for you have all the guides about whom the warriors spoke to you. They will take you over and take care of you. Well, we have told you a good road to take. If anyone tells a falsehood in speaking of the spirit-road, you will fall off the bridge and be burned. However you need not worry for you will pass over safely. As you proceed from that place the spirits will come to meet you and take you to the village where the chief lives. There you will give him the tobacco and ask for those objects of which we spoke to you, the same you asked of the old woman. There you will meet all the relatives that died before you. They will be living in a large lodge. This you must enter.

> —An oral tradition of the
> Winnebago tribe of Wisconsin

———❦———

*This Maori story relates that a woman died and returned to life.
She was able to recount her experience of the afterworld, which has
a distinct physical location in the direction of the North Cape of New
Zealand. Her relatives are disappointed at the end of the story because
she was not able to retain any physical evidence of her journey,
although they accept her story as true nonetheless.*

This story was told to Mr. Shortland by a servant
of his named Te Wharewera. An aunt of this man died
in a solitary hut near the banks of Lake Rotorua. Being
a lady of rank she was left in her hut, the door and
windows were made fast, and the dwelling was abandoned, as her death had made it *tapu*. But a day or two
after, Te Wharewera with some others paddling in a
canoe near the place at early morning saw a figure on the
shore beckoning to them. It was the aunt come back to
life again, but weak and cold, and famished. When suf-
ficiently restored by their timely help, she told her story.
Leaving her body, her spirit had taken the flight toward
the North Cape, and arrived at the entrance of Reigna.
There, holding on by the stem of the creeping akeake-
plant, she descended the precipice, and found herself on
the sandy beach of a river. Looking around, she espied
in the distance an enormous bird, taller than a man, coming towards her with rapid strides. This terrible object
so frightened her, that her first thought was to try to

return up the steep cliff; but seeing an old man paddling a small canoe towards her she ran to meet him, and so escaped the bird. When she had been safely ferried across she asked the old Charon, mentioning the name of her family, where the spirits of her kindred dwelt. Following the path the man pointed out, she was surprised to find it just such a path as she had been used to on earth; the aspect of the country, the trees, shrubs, and plants were all familiar to her. She reached the village and among the crowd assembled there she found her father and many near relations; they saluted her, and welcomed her with the wailing chant which Maoris always address to people met after long absence. But when her father had asked about his living relatives, and especially about her own child, he told her she must go back to earth, for no one was left to take care of his grandchild. By his orders she refused to touch the food that the dead people offered her, and in spite of their efforts to detain her, her father got her safely into the canoe, crossed with her, and parting gave her from under his cloak two enormous sweet potatoes to plant at home for his grandchild's especial eating. But as she began to climb the precipice again, two pursuing infant spirits pulled her back, and she only escaped by flinging the roots on them, which they stopped to eat, while she scaled the rock by help of the akeake-stem, till she reached the earth and flew back to where she had left her body. On returning to life she found herself in darkness, and what had passed seemed as a

dream, till she perceived that she was deserted and the
door fast, and concluded that she really had died and
come to life again. When morning dawned, a faint light
entered by the crevices of the shut-up house, and she saw
on the floor near her a calabash partly full of red ochre
mixed with water; this she eagerly drained to the dregs,
and then feeling a little stronger, succeeded in opening
the door and crawling down to the beach, where her
friends soon after found her. Those who listened to her
tale firmly believed the reality of her adventures, but it
was much regretted that she had not brought back at
least one of the huge sweet potatoes, as evidence of her
visit to the land of spirits.

—A tale of the Maori of New Zealand

*The Guajiro Indians of Venezuela tell this story, of a man who was
reunited with his wife in the land of the spirits. He is unhappy with
her behavior in that land, because the habits of the spirits are very
different from the habits of the living. He is eventually compelled to
return to the land of the living without her.*

A Guajiro Indian wept so long,
so long for his dead wife
that she took pity on him.

The Watch-House of the Sun

One night she came to him,
in a dream.
She looked human.
She seemed to be alive.

She came toward him..
"My wife! My wife! Stop!
I am here! Don't leave me!"
cried the Guajiro, rising to his feet.
She did not answer.
Going past him, she quickened her step.

At dawn
they found themselves by a mountain.
Here was where the woman lived.
Before reaching the summit,
they passed over shifting, muddy ground,
over a land in which one sinks.

Drunken talk could be heard.
A bull bellowed, goats bleated:
they had been eaten at a dead man's burial.
And on dead horses drunken yolujas galloped.
When they arrived,
when the sun had risen,
the long-dead hailed the Guajiro.
"Brother-in-law!" said one.

"How are you, friend?" asked another.
"Cousin!" exclaimed a third.

The Guajiro alone still looked like a living man.
There they ate muskmelon and watermelon.
Each morning
a pot with cooked food awaited him.

Thus for many days, he stayed with her.

"They have come to take me dancing,
but you stay here!" she said to him one day.
A yonna dance has been organized.
All the yolujas were invited.
"I'm coming with you!" said the Guajiro.
He went to follow her.
"They'll do things to me there you wouldn't like to
        see!"

The place where the ball was being held was lit up.
A large number of people dressed in red were
        dancing.
Everything appeared red.
Someone was playing a drum.

"Wait for me here!" said the woman.
But the Guajiro insisted on following her.

The Watch-House of the Sun

Together they went on to another house.
"Now you stay here! I'll bring you food!"

This time the Guajiro let her go.

Immediately afterward,
some young men came up to her.
They embraced her.
They kissed her on the mouth.

The Guajiro had moved forward to get a better
        view.
He was very shocked.
He turned round and went back toward the house.

The woman changed her dress,
and started to dance again.

                    —A poem of the Guajiro tribe

—————

*The Warao Indians of Venezuela believe in a sky-heaven. Its dis-
covery is preserved in this story, which also explains the Warao custom
of leaving food and water on the grave.*

In early times when all Indians lived in just one village, they began to die in succession, one after another.
It was night and the Indians, gathered in the house of

the patriarch, were commenting on the situation, "If we keep on dying like this, very soon we will all be gone."

When they spoke like this, a great white bird appeared to them in the air. And upon soaring in flight, he said to them, "Don't think that only I have died. You also will go on dying after me." And it kept on rising to the clouds. When they saw that it was going, the Indians cried to it, "Come back and stay with us. Don't climb to the heavens." But the soul continued rising in the atmosphere, in the form of a bird, contented and singing.

It repeated, "I am going, I am going above where my companions are waiting for me. I have lived enough on the earth. Now I have found a land much more beautiful and desirable than that world below." Afterwards it added, "There I will live forever in company with other Indians, because even though we die one after the other, there we get together in the same place."

Another day the Indians saw that in an abandoned village all the souls of the dead of that place had gotten together, and they were crying because their friends and relatives had put out neither water to drink nor food on the grave. For that reason they were thirsty and hungry. From this event comes the custom that the Warao observe of putting water and food on the grave or coffin, and also on the road that leads to the grave.

—An oral tradition of the Warao

The Watch-House of the Sun

The Ge Indians of Brazil tell this story of a party of hunters who stumbled across the land of the spirits. There is no violence there, as attested to by the inability of the hunters to kill the unusual beast they discover. Further, the Ge custom of dancing is retained in the afterlife.

In the extreme east of the old Ramkokamekra area there is a lake in the steppe called Lagoa Formosa by the Neobrazilians. At one time there was an island in the lake that constantly shifted its position. On it was standing a pindahiba tree, which inclined hither and thither till its top would nearly touch the level of the water.

Once a band of hunters moved past near the lake and saw a queer animal walking along the steppe by the lake. It resembled somewhat the great anteater. At once one of the hunters pursued the animal, ready to shoot, but when he got near it his companions noted with amazement that he removed the arrow from the string, which he took off the stave and wrapped around the tip of his bow; then he shouldered the bow, and peaceably walked on with the beast. At once two other hunters, their weapons in readiness, pursued the animal and the man, but with the same result. As soon as they had caught up they lowered their weapons, took them under their arms, and quietly walked beside the animal, which marched toward the lake with its three companions, and all together vanished from the sight of the hunting party.

Later, a band of Ramkokamekra were again hunting in the vicinity of the lake and camped by its shore. Suddenly they saw an Indian carrying a slain deer on his back toward the lagoon. They thought he wanted to drink there, but he entered the water and disappeared. Soon they heard a noise below the water, then the sound of a dance rattle, and of dancers; after a while the noise died away. At the hour of nocturnal dancing the sound was heard again, and once more before dawn. Then the hunters in alarm abandoned the site, for they recognized that the lake was the dwelling of the souls of the dead.

—An oral tradition of the Ge

This story from the Chamacoco Indians of Argentina describes the physical structure of the heavens. Heaven itself is a place of light, and from it the shaman in the story learns the magic required to cure disease.

Pintura was a shaman. When his wife died he cried every night. Once he was very sleepy, and a man took him up to Nemourt, traveling past this sky which you see, to a more distant sky called poort yetit. He showed Pintura how that other sky was quite close to ours. It was drizzling in that upper sky, but it was a rain of fire, falling stones, but like fire.

Up there he was taken to the first, the second, and the third sky, and then the man showed him the shower of fire. There he stayed, with Nemourt. That sky, the yetit, is also called the "different sky." The first sky is called the "yellow sky," and the second the "blue sky."

Pintura stared all around him. He looked at the falling rain, which was like fire, very cold, but burning like fire. Up there Nemourt gave him his magic power so that he would be stronger than the other shamans; he gave him power so he would know everything he could know. And he did what Nemourt told him to do.

Pintura saw many people up in that sky, and after a while they got to know him and they became friends. Those people ruled yetit. When he dreamed he saw them with their ropes of braided hair and their rhea feathers. There were no Indians among them; they were the diseases which live up in the third sky, and they looked almost like white foreigners. Nemourt spoke to Pintura. He showed him the diseases, and let him see how they were all shamans, pulling a disease from their mouths and throwing it down to the earth. He also showed him how the sickness is extracted with a finger, pressing and pulling where it hurts. He told him that those diseases descend to earth on the wind. Finally Nemourt said that the shaman was going to become like the other shamans in the third sky. He seized the man, spat into his hand,

and told him what to do in order to obtain magic power. Pintura cupped his hands into which Nemourt spat and then made the other rub his own body; thus he gave the man magic power to control disease. Those diseases had to descend to earth on the wind.

In the third sky there was brilliant light. When a disease comes close the light catches it and kills it. The light, which is called dolayo, hangs over each shaman in order to protect him from disease; it sees the disease and knows what kind it is.

—An oral tradition of the Chamacoco

———

This legend from the Tonga people of Melanesia situates heaven on a physical island, kept safe from invasion by the living by its unusual air. The island is distinguished by the absence of death; as soon as anything perishes, it is restored to life immediately.

With regard to the fate of the soul after death, the Tongans universally and positively believed in the existence of a great island, lying at a considerable distance to the northwest, which they considered to be the abode of their gods and of the souls of their dead nobles and their ministers. This island they supposed to be much larger than all the other islands put together, and to be well stocked with all kinds of useful and ornamental plants, always in a high state of perfection, and always bearing the richest fruits and the most beautiful flowers according to their respective natures; they thought that when these fruits or flowers were plucked, others immediately took their place, and that the whole atmosphere was filled with the most delightful fragrance that the imagination can conceive, exhaled from these immortal plants. The island, too, was well stocked with the most beautiful birds, of all imaginable kinds, as well as with abundance of hogs; and all of these creatures were immortal, except when they were killed to provide food for the gods. But the moment a hog or bird was killed, another live hog or bird came into existence to supply its place, just as happened with the fruits and flowers; and this, so far as they could ascertain, was the only way in which plants and animals were propagated in Bolotoo. So far away was the happy island supposed to be that it was dangerou for living men to attempt to sail thither in their canoes; indeed, except by the express permission of the gods, they could not find the island, however near they might come to it. They tell, however, of a Tongan canoe which, returning from Fiji, was driven by stress of weather to Bolotoo. The crew knew not the place, and being in want of provisions and seeing the country to abound in all sorts of fruits, they landed and proceeded to pluck some bread-fruit. But to their unspeakable astonishment they could no more lay hold of the fruit than if it were a shadow; they walked through the trunks of the trees and passed through the substance of the houses without feeling any shock or resistance. At length they saw some of the gods, who passed through the men's bodies as if they were empty space. These gods recommended them to go away immediately, as they had no proper food for them, and they promised them a fair wind and a speedy passage. So the men put to sea, and sailing with the utmost speed they arrived at Samoa, where they stayed two or three days. Thence, again sailing very fast, they returned to Tonga, where in the course of a few days they all died, not as a punishment for having been at Bolotoo, but as a natural consequence, the air of that place, as it were, infecting mortal bodies with a speedy death. The gods who dwell in Bolotoo have no canoes, not requiring them; for if they wish to be anywhere, there they are the moment the wish is felt.

—An oral tradition of the Tonga

ACKNOWLEDGMENTS

Pages 11–13: From *Miracles: A Preliminary Study* by C. S. Lewis © 1974 Macmillan Co.

Pages 15–17: From *The Last Battle* by C. S. Lewis, © 1956 Macmillan Co.

Page 22: Copyright © 1989 by Italica Press. From Eileen Gardiner, *Visions of Heaven and Hell before Dante*. New York: Italica Press, 1989. By permission of Italica Press.

Pages 35–38: From Brock, Sebastian, trans. *Hymns on Paradise*. Copyright © 1990 St. Vladimir's Seminary Press.

Pages 38–42: From Palmer, G.E.H., et al., trans. *The Philokalia: The Complete Text*, Volumes II and IV. London: Faber and Faber Ltd., 1981. By permission of Faber and Faber Ltd.

Pages 52–53: Approximately 150 words from *Twilight of the Idols/The Anti-Christ* by Friedrich Nietzsche, translated by R. J. Hollingdale.

(Penguin Classics 1968, Second edition 1990). Translation copyright © R. J. Hollingdale, 1968. Reprinted by permission of Penguin Books Ltd.

Pages 61–66: From Epstein, I., ed. *The Soncino Talmud*. London: Soncino Press. By permission of Soncino Press.

Pages 74–75: From Kaplan, Aryeh, trans. *The Bahir*. Copyright © 1979 Samuel Wiser, Inc. Reprinted by permission of the publisher.

Pages 75–76: From *Safed Spirituality* by Lawrence Fine © 1984 by Lawrence Fine. Reprinted by permission of Paulist Press.

Pages 77–80: From *Jewish Mystical Testimonies* by Louis Jacobs © 1976 Schocken Books.

Page 91–92: From Rowson, Everett K. *A Muslim Philosopher on the Soul and Its Fate*. New Haven: American Oriental Society, 1988. By permission of the American Oriental Society.

Pages 95–97: *The Precious Pearl: A Translation from the Arabic with Notes of the* Kitāb al-Durra al-Fākhira fī Kashf ʿUlūm al-Ākhira *of Abū Hamid Muhammad b. Muhammad b. Muhammad al-Ghazālī*, trans. and ed. Jane Idleman Smith. Studies in World Religions, no. 1. Cambridge, Mass.: Harvard University Center for the Study of World Religions, 1979, pp. 73–75.

Pages 105–106: From *The Tibetan Book of the Dead* by Francesca Fremantle and Chogyam Trungpa © 1975. Reprinted by arrangement with Shambhala Publications, Inc., Boston.

Pages 109–111: From *Three Worlds According to King Ruang*, Frank and Mani Reynolds, trans., © 1982, University of California Center for South and Southeast Asian Studies.

UCLA Latin American Center, 1987, pp. 40–41. Reprinted by permission of The Regents of the University of California.

Pages 184–186: From *The Belief in Immortality and the Worship of the Dead* by Sir James Frazer, © 1922, Macmillan and Co., London. Reprinted by permission of A. P. Watt Ltd. on behalf of the Council of Trinity College, Cambridge.